Crocheted Cats

Crocheted Cats

10 FELINE FRIENDS TO CROCHET

VANESSA MOONCIE

132

90

18

78

146

104

Contents

Introduction

This book contains a collection of ten crocheted cat patterns. Some are domestic cats, such as the Black and White, and others are pedigree breeds, including a Bengal and the large Maine Coon. There are six patterns for standing cats along with instructions for a sleeping Russian Blue and a Ginger cat, and sitting Siamese and Calico cats.

The projects are worked mainly in rounds and rows of double crochet, but other stitches are used to create distinguishing features. The fluffy coat of the Ragdoll cat is worked in loop stitch, while half treble and treble stitches form the shaping at the front of the Exotic Shorthair cat's face. All of the projects are crocheted in double-knit yarn. The written instructions are accompanied by charts to make it easy to follow the patterns.

The projects are designed to suit all levels, from the beginner to the experienced crocheter. At the back of the book are sections on getting started, illustrated step-by-step instructions for the crochet stitches used, joining in new colours, sewing the cats together and adding the embroidered finishing touches.

Cats have been part of our family for the last 25 years or so. They were all domestic shorthairs and all had very different characters. These patterns can be adapted to create portraits of your own family cat, sleeping, sitting or standing.

Vanessa Mooncie

Black and White Cat

Bengal

Maine Coon

Siamese

Exotic Shorthair

Calico Cat

Ginger Cat

Ragdoll

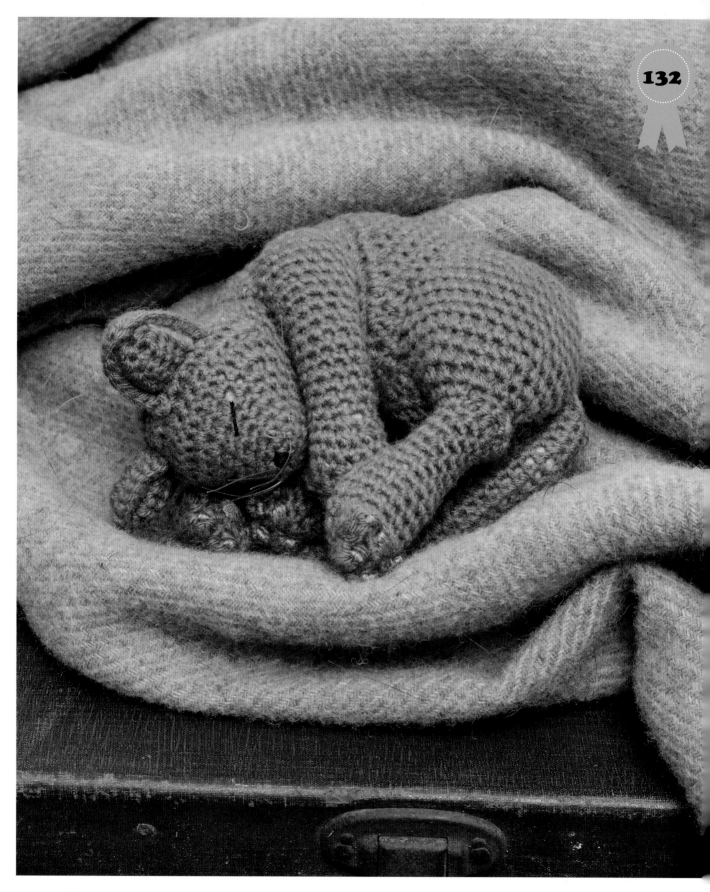

Russian Blue

American Bobtail

Black and White Cat

THIS BLACK AND WHITE CAT IS CROCHETED USING SIMPLE COLOUR CHANGES TO FORM THE TUXEDO MARKINGS. A TOUCH OF PINK IS USED FOR THE INNER EARS AND EMBROIDERED NOSE.

Materials

- Stylecraft Naturals Bamboo and Cotton, 60% bamboo, 40% cotton (273yd/250m per 100g ball), or any DK yarn:
  1 x 100g ball in 7127 Chalk (A)
  1 x 100g ball in 7153 Pitch (B)
  1 x 100g ball in 7165 Rose (C)
- Stranded embroidery thread in green, such as Anchor Stranded Cotton, shade 0265, for the eyes
- Stranded embroidery thread in black, such as Anchor Stranded Cotton, shade 0403, for the pupils
- 6 lengths of 0.3mm clear nylon thread, each measuring 4¾in (12cm), for the optional whiskers (not suitable for young children)
- 3.25mm (UK10:USD/3) crochet hook
- Blunt-ended yarn needle
- Toy stuffing
- Stitch marker

Size

- Approximately 6¾in (17cm) body length, from tip of nose to back of hind legs
- Approximately 6in (15cm) tall from top of head (excluding ears)

Tension

23 sts and 24 rows to 4in (10cm) over double crochet using 3.25mm hook. Use a larger or smaller hook if necessary to obtain the correct tension.

Method

The cat's head, body and legs are worked in rounds and rows of double crochet, using two colours. The neck is worked in rows, using two colours, starting by crocheting into the stitches at the underside of the muzzle, and then along the edges of the rows that make up the top of the head. The ears are worked in rows. Each ear is made up of two crocheted parts that are joined by crocheting into each stitch of both pieces at the same time. Double crochet and half treble stitches form the tapered shape of the tail. The stitches are decreased in the last row to form a curve in the tail. The long edges of the tail are sewn together and a small amount of stuffing is inserted before sewing it in place. The legs are worked in continuous rounds of double crochet. The toes on the paws are produced by crocheting bobbles. The bobbles appear on the reverse side of the fabric, so the work is turned after crocheting the toes and continued on the right side. The eyes and nose are embroidered with embroidery threads and yarn.

1 ch and 2 ch at beg of the row/round does not count as a st throughout.

Head

Starting at front of muzzle, with 3.25mm hook and A, make a magic loop (see page 163).

Round 1: 1 ch, 6 dc into loop (6 sts).
Round 2 (inc): (Dc2inc) 6 times (12 sts). Pull tightly on short end of yarn to close loop.
Rounds 3–4: 1 dc in each dc.
Round 5: (Dc2inc, 1 dc) 6 times. Join B in last dc and carry unused yarn on WS of work (18 sts).

SHAPE FACE

The following is worked in rows.
Row 1 (RS): 1 dc in next 13 dc with B, with A work 1 dc in next 5 dc, turn.
Row 2 (WS) (inc): 1 ch, 1 dc in next 5 dc with A; with B, 1 dc in next dc, (dc2inc, 1 dc) 6 times, sl st to first dc, turn (24 sts).
Row 3 (inc): With B, 1 dc in next 3 dc, (dc2inc, 2 dc) 5 times, 1 dc in next dc, finishing 5 sts before the end, turn (29 sts).

HEAD
ROUNDS 1–5

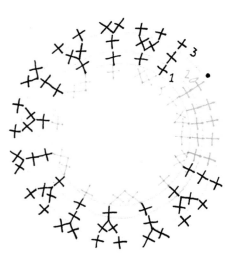

SHAPE FACE
ROWS 1–3

KEY

⟳ MAGIC LOOP

𝒪 CHAIN (CH)

• SLIP STITCH (SL ST)

+ DOUBLE CROCHET (DC)

✕✕ DC2INC

⁑✕ DC3INC

✕✕ DC2TOG

⊤ HALF TREBLE (HTR)

⋏ HTR2TOG

⊕ MAKE BOBBLE (MB)

TOP OF HEAD

Continue with B.

Row 4 (WS): 1 ch, 1 dc in next 24 dc, turn.

Continue on these 24 sts.

Row 5 (RS): 1 ch, 1 dc in each dc, turn.

Rows 6–8: Rep last row.

Row 9 (dec): 1 ch, (dc2tog, 2 dc) 6 times, turn (18 sts).

Row 10 (dec): 1 ch, (dc2tog, 1 dc) 6 times, turn (12 sts).

Row 11 (dec): 1 ch, (dc2tog) 6 times (6 sts).

Fasten off B and thread through last 6 stitches. Pull tightly on end of yarn and fasten off. Do not fasten off A.

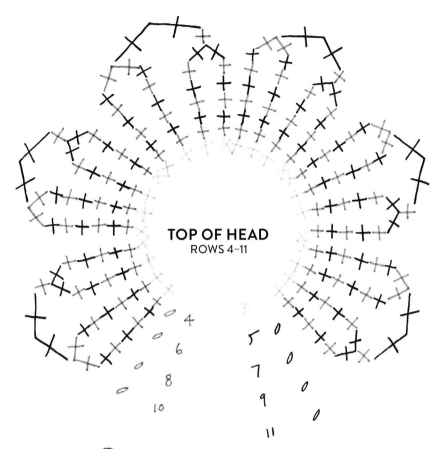

TOP OF HEAD
ROWS 4–11

COLOUR KEY FOR YARNS

FOR SHAPE FACE, NECK & SHAPE MIDDLE OF BODY

All other charts are shown in alternate rounds/rows of blue and black.

NECK

With RS of head facing, 3.25mm hook and A, sl st to first of unworked 5 dc of row 2 of shape face.

Row 1 (RS): 1 dc in same st as sl st, 1 dc in next 4 dc. Join B in last dc and carry unused yarn on WS of work. With B, work 14 dc evenly along edge of the rows of head, sl st to first dc, turn (19 sts).

Row 2 (WS) (inc): 1 dc in next dc, dc2inc, 1 dc in next 10 dc, dc2inc, 1 dc in next dc with B; with A, (dc2inc, 1 dc) twice, dc2inc, turn (24 sts).

Row 3: With A, 1 ch, 1 dc in next 8 dc; with B, 1 dc in next 16 dc, sl st to first dc, turn.

Row 4: With B, 1 dc in next 16 dc; with A, 1 dc in next 8 dc, sl st to first dc, turn.

Row 5: 1 dc in next 8 dc with A. Sl st to next st and fasten off, leaving a long tail each of A and B.

NECK
ROWS 1–5

Ears (make 2)

With 3.25mm hook and C, make 4 ch.

Row 1: 1 dc in 2nd ch from hook, 1 dc in next ch, 3 dc in next ch, 1 dc in reverse side of next 2 ch, turn (7 sts).

Row 2 (inc): 1 ch, dc2inc, 1 dc in next 2 dc, dc3inc, 1 dc in next 2 dc, dc2inc (11 sts).

Fasten off, leaving a long tail of yarn. This completes the inner ear.

With B, make one more piece to match the first for the outer ear. Turn work at the end and do not fasten off.

Body

SHAPE FRONT

Starting at front of body, with 3.25mm hook and A, make 10 ch.

Row 1 (RS): 1 dc in 2nd ch from hook, 1 dc in next 7 ch, 2 dc in end ch, 1 dc in reverse side of next 8 ch, turn (18 sts). Place a marker on the first stitch to mark the top of the front of the body.

Row 2 (WS) (inc): 1 ch, (dc2inc, 2 dc)

JOIN EAR PIECES

Place the two ear pieces together, with the inner ear facing up.

Next: 1 ch, inserting the hook under both loops of each stitch of the inner ear first, then the outer ear at the same time to join, dc2inc, 1 dc in next 4 dc, dc3inc, 1 dc in next 4 dc, dc2inc (15 sts). Fasten off, leaving a long tail of yarn.

6 times, sl st to first dc, turn (24 sts).

Row 3 (inc): (Dc2inc, 3 dc) 6 times, turn (30 sts).

Row 4 (inc): 1 ch, (dc2inc, 4 dc) 6 times, sl st to first dc, turn (36 sts).

Row 5: 1 dc in next 24 dc. Join B in last dc. With B, work 1 dc in next 12 dc, do not turn.

Next (RS): With B, work 1 dc in next 12 dc, turn.

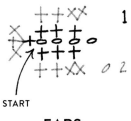

EARS
ROWS 1–2

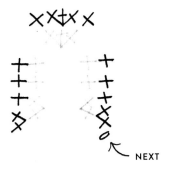

JOIN EAR PIECES
INSERT HOOK INTO EACH
STITCH OF BOTH EAR PIECES
AT SAME TIME TO JOIN

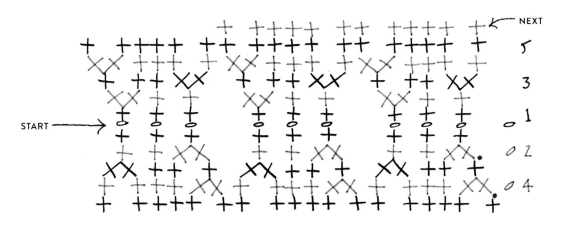

SHAPE FRONT
ROWS 1–5 & NEXT

SHAPE MIDDLE OF BODY

Row 1 (WS): 1 ch, 1 dc in next 24 dc with B, 1 dc in next 12 dc with A, sl st to first dc, turn.

Row 2 (RS): 1 dc in next 12 dc with A, 1 dc in next 24 dc with B, turn.

Rows 3–18: Rep rows 1–2 8 times.

REP ROWS 1-2

3 — 18

2

1

SHAPE MIDDLE
OF BODY
ROWS 1–18

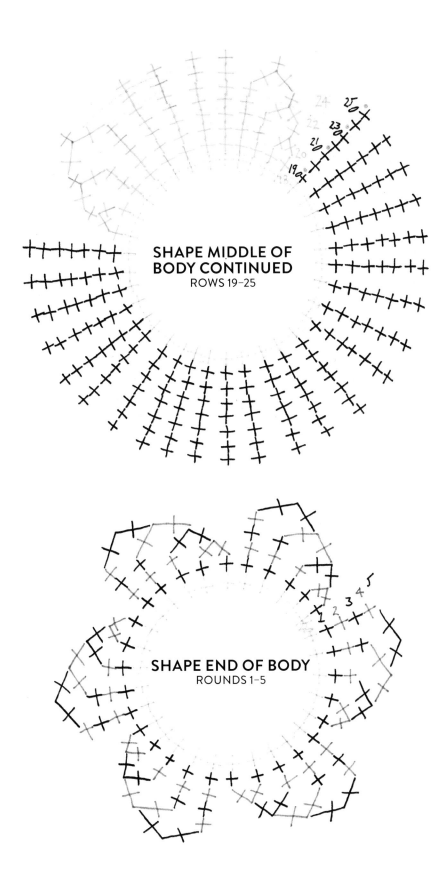

SHAPE MIDDLE OF BODY CONTINUED
ROWS 19–25

SHAPE END OF BODY
ROUNDS 1–5

Row 19: Rep row 1.

Row 20 (dec): With A, dc2tog, 1 dc in next 8 dc, dc2tog, 1 dc in next 24 dc with B, turn (34 sts).

Row 21: 1 ch, 1 dc in next 24 dc with B, 1 dc in next 10 dc with A, sl st to first dc, turn.

Row 22 (dec): With A, dc2tog, 1 dc in next 6 dc, dc2tog, 1 dc in next 24 dc with B, turn (32 sts).

Row 23: 1 ch, 1 dc in next 24 dc with B, 1 dc in next 8 dc with A, sl st to first dc, turn.

Row 24 (dec): With A, dc2tog, 1 dc in next 4 dc, dc2tog, 1 dc in next 24 dc with B, turn (30 sts).

Row 25: 1 ch, 1 dc in next 24 dc with B, 1 dc in next 6 dc with A, sl st to first dc, turn.

SHAPE END OF BODY

The following is worked in rounds. Continue with B.

Round 1: 1 dc in each dc.

Round 2 (dec): (Dc2tog, 3 dc) 6 times (24 sts).

Stuff body before continuing.

Round 3 (dec): (Dc2tog, 2 dc) 6 times (18 sts).

Round 4 (dec): (Dc2tog, 1 dc) 6 times (12 sts).

Round 5 (dec): (Dc2tog) 6 times (6 sts).

Break yarn and thread through last 6 stitches. Pull tightly on end of yarn to close. Fasten off.

Front legs (make 2)

The bobbles appear on the reverse
side of the work. This will be the
right side. See page 166 for
instructions to make bobble (mb).
Starting at the base of the paw,
with 3.25mm hook and A, make
a magic loop.

Round 1 (WS): 1 ch, 6 dc into loop
(6 sts).

Round 2 (inc): (Dc2inc) 6 times
(12 sts). Pull tightly on short end of
yarn to close loop.

Round 3 (inc): (Dc2inc, 2 dc) 4 times
(16 sts).

Round 4: 1 dc in next 8 dc, (mb, 1 dc
in next dc) 4 times, turn.

Round 5 (RS) (dec): 1 ch, 1 dc in first
dc, (1 dc in next st, dc2tog) twice,
1 dc in next 9 dc (14 sts).

Round 6 (dec): (1 dc in next dc,
dc2tog) twice, 1 dc in next 8 dc
(12 sts).

Round 7: 1 dc in each dc. Join B in
last dc.
Continue with B.

Rounds 8–12: 1 dc in each dc.

Round 13 (inc): (Dc2inc, 3 dc) 3 times
(15 sts).

Rounds 14–17: 1 dc in each dc.

Round 18 (inc): (Dc2inc, 4 dc) 3 times
(18 sts).

Rounds 19–23: 1 dc in each dc.
Stuff leg before continuing.

Round 24 (dec): (Dc2tog, 1 dc)
6 times (12 sts).

Round 25 (dec): (Dc2tog) 6 times
(6 sts).

Break yarn and thread through
last round of stitches. Pull tightly
on end of yarn to close. Fasten off,
leaving a long tail of B at the end.

FRONT LEGS
ROUNDS 1–4

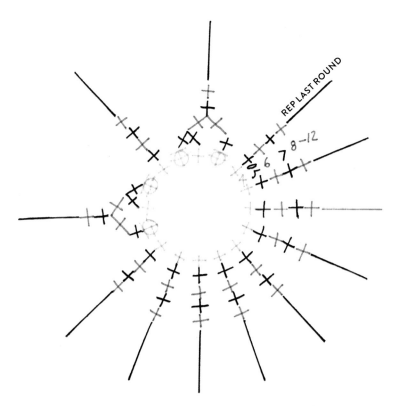

**FRONT LEGS
CONTINUED**
ROUNDS 5–12

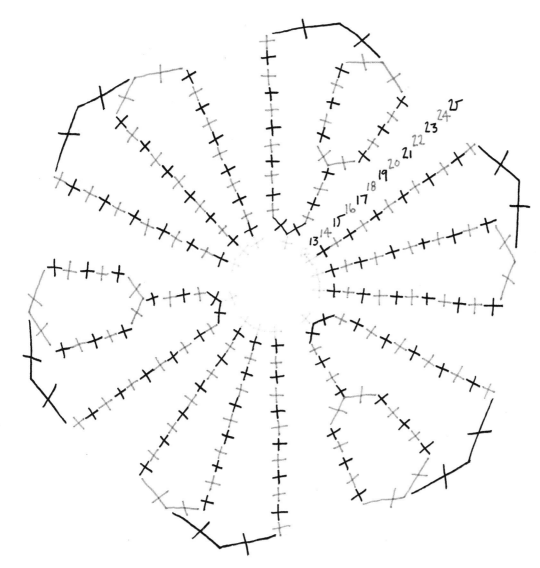

FRONT LEGS CONTINUED
ROUNDS 13–25

Hind legs (make 2)

Starting at the base of the paw, with 3.25mm hook and A, make a magic loop.

Rounds 1–12: Work as for rounds 1–12 of front legs, using A throughout.

SHAPE BACK OF LEG

Round 13: 1 dc in next dc, ending at the side of the leg; 6 ch, skip the 6 dc at the front of the leg, 1 dc in next 5 dc.

Round 14: 1 dc in next dc, 1 dc in next 6 ch, 1 dc in next 5 dc. Break yarn and thread through last round of stitches. Pull tightly on end of yarn to close and fasten off.

HIND LEGS
SHAPE BACK OF LEG
ROUNDS 13–14

SHAPE THIGH

With RS of leg facing, 3.25mm hook, and A, sl st in first of skipped 6 dc of round 12.

Round 1: 1 dc in same st as sl st, 1 dc in next 5 dc, 1 dc in reverse side of next 6 ch (12 sts).

Round 2: 1 dc in each dc. Join B in last dc.

Continue with B.

Round 3 (inc): (Dc2inc, 1 dc) 6 times (18 sts).

Rounds 4–6: 1 dc in each dc.

Round 7 (inc): (Dc2inc, 2 dc) 6 times (24 sts).

Rounds 8–10: 1 dc in each dc.

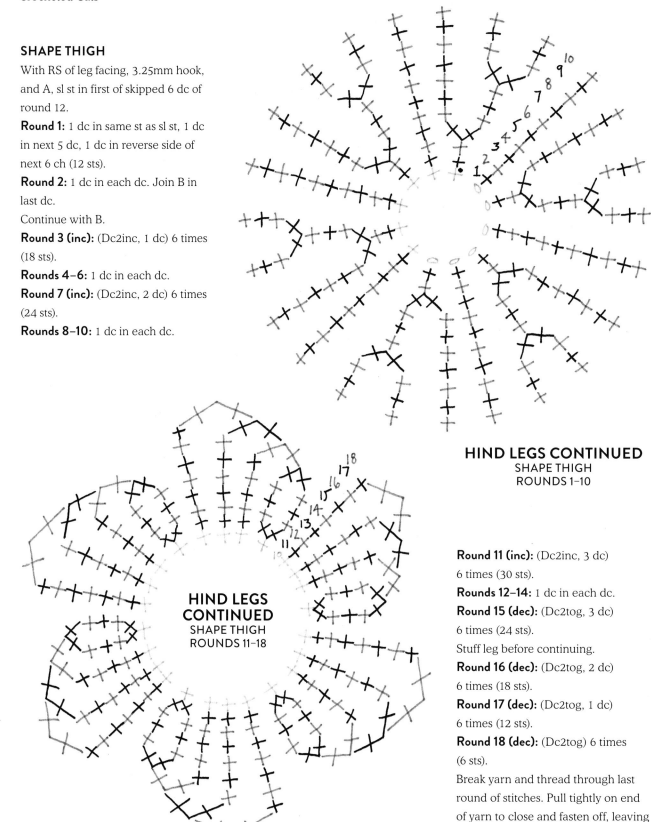

HIND LEGS CONTINUED
SHAPE THIGH
ROUNDS 1–10

Round 11 (inc): (Dc2inc, 3 dc) 6 times (30 sts).

Rounds 12–14: 1 dc in each dc.

Round 15 (dec): (Dc2tog, 3 dc) 6 times (24 sts).

Stuff leg before continuing.

Round 16 (dec): (Dc2tog, 2 dc) 6 times (18 sts).

Round 17 (dec): (Dc2tog, 1 dc) 6 times (12 sts).

Round 18 (dec): (Dc2tog) 6 times (6 sts).

Break yarn and thread through last round of stitches. Pull tightly on end of yarn to close and fasten off, leaving a long tail of B at the end.

HIND LEGS CONTINUED
SHAPE THIGH
ROUNDS 11–18

TAIL

With 3.25mm hook and A, make 31 ch.

Row 1: 1 dc in 2nd ch from hook, 1 dc in next 28 ch, 3 dc in end ch, 1 dc in reverse side of next 29 ch, turn (61 sts).

Row 2 (dec): 2 ch, 1 htr in next 10 dc, (htr2tog, 1 htr) 4 times, 1 dc in next 8 dc, dc3inc, 1 dc in next 8 dc, (1 htr, htr2tog) 4 times, 1 htr in next 10 dc (55 sts).

Fasten off, leaving a long tail of yarn at the end.

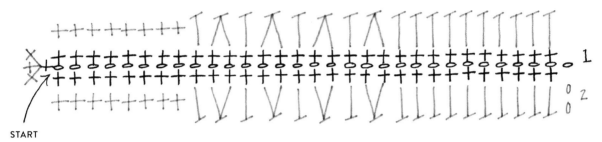

TAIL
ROWS 1–2

Making up

HEAD

Stuff the head. With the tails of yarn left after fastening off, sew the head in place, indicated by the marker at the top of the body. Stitch all around the neck edges. Insert more stuffing into the neck if necessary. Using three strands of embroidery thread, embroider the pupils of the eyes in satin stitch and work straight stitches around each eye to form the irises (see page 170). With C, embroider the nose in satin stitch.

EARS

Stuff the ears lightly, keeping them flat. Sew the ears in place, near the back of the head, stitching all around the lower edges with the tails of yarn left after fastening off.

LEGS

Flatten the top of the legs and sew in place, stitching all around the top of the thighs with the tail of yarn left after fastening off.

TAIL

Using the length of yarn left after fastening off, fold the tail lengthways and sew the long edges together with whip stitch (see page 169). Use the end of the crochet hook to push a small amount of stuffing into the tail. Sew the tail in place.

WHISKERS (OPTIONAL)

Attach three whiskers to the posts of the stitches on each side of the muzzle (see page 171). Trim the ends. Weave in all the yarn ends.

Bengal

MULTIPLE COLOUR CHANGES ARE USED TO CREATE THE LEOPARD PRINT AND STRIPED DESIGN ON THIS BENGAL CAT'S COAT.

Materials

- King Cole Merino DK, 100% merino superwash (153yd/140m per 50g ball), or any DK yarn:
  1 x 50g ball in 2612 Cream (A)
  1 x 50g ball in 3327 Pebble (B)
  1 x 50g ball in 2636 Chocolate (C)
  1 x 50g ball in 2629 Gingerbread (D)
- Stranded embroidery thread in green, such as Anchor Stranded Cotton, shade 0215, for the eyes
- Stranded embroidery thread in black, such as Anchor Stranded Cotton, shade 0403, for the pupils
- Stranded embroidery thread in pink/brown, such as Anchor Stranded Cotton, shade 0883, for the nose
- 6 lengths of 0.3mm clear nylon thread, each measuring 4¾in (12cm), for the optional whiskers (not suitable for young children)
- 3.25mm (UK10:USD/3) crochet hook
- Blunt-ended yarn needle
- Toy stuffing

Size

- Approximately 8¼in (21cm) body length, from tip of nose to back of hind legs
- Approximately 6¾in (17cm) tall from top of head (excluding ears)

Tension

22 sts and 24 rows to 4in (10cm) over double crochet using 3.25mm hook. Use a larger or smaller hook if necessary to obtain the correct tension.

Method

The Bengal cat's head, body and legs are worked in rounds and rows of double crochet, using four colours to create the pattern of the cat's coat. The neck is worked in rows, using three colours. It is started by crocheting into the stitches at the underside of the muzzle, and then along the edges of the rows that make up the top of the head. The ears are worked in rows. Each ear is made up of two crocheted parts that are joined by crocheting into each stitch of both pieces at the same time. Double crochet and half treble stitches produce the curve in the tail, worked in two alternating colour stripes. The toes on the paws are made by crocheting bobbles that appear on the reverse side of the fabric. The eyes and nose are embroidered with stranded embroidery threads.

1 ch and 2 ch at beg of the row/round does not count as a st throughout.

Head

Starting at front of muzzle, with 3.25mm hook and A, make a magic loop (see page 163).

Round 1: 1 ch, 6 dc into loop (6 sts).

Round 2 (inc): (Dc2inc) 6 times, join B in last dc and carry unused yarn on WS of work. (12 sts). Pull tightly on short end of A to close loop.

SHAPE FACE

The following is worked in rows.

Row 1 (RS): 1 dc in next 8 dc with B, 1 dc in next 4 dc with A, turn.

Row 2 (WS): 1 ch, 1 dc in next 4 dc with A, 1 dc in next 8 dc with B, sl st to first dc, turn.

Row 3 (inc): Dc2inc with B. Join C in last dc; 1 dc in next dc with C; with B, dc2inc, 1 dc in next 2 dc, dc2inc; with C, 1 dc in next dc; with B, dc2inc; with A, 1 dc in next dc, (dc2inc) twice, 1 dc in next dc, turn (18 sts).

Row 4 (WS) (inc): With A, 1 ch, 1 dc in next 6 dc; with B, dc2inc, 1 dc in next dc; dc2inc with C, (1 dc, dc2inc, 1 dc) twice with B, dc2inc with C; with B, 1 dc in next dc, dc2inc, sl st to first dc, turn (24 sts).

Row 5 (inc): Dc2inc, 1 dc in next dc with B, 1 dc in next 2 dc with C, (1 dc, dc2inc) twice with B, 1 dc in next 2 dc with C, (dc2inc, 1 dc) twice with B, 1 dc in next 2 dc with C; with B, 1 dc in next dc, dc2inc, finishing 6 sts before the end, turn (30 sts).

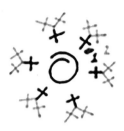

HEAD
ROUNDS 1–2

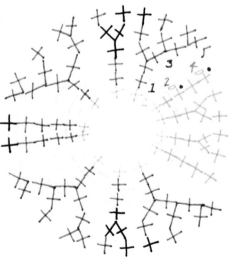

SHAPE FACE
ROWS 1–5

KEY

⊙ MAGIC LOOP

↗ CHAIN (CH)

• SLIP STITCH (SL ST)

+ DOUBLE CROCHET (DC)

⤬⤬ DC2INC

⤬⤬ DC3INC

⤬⤬ DC2TOG

↑ HALF TREBLE (HTR)

⊕ MAKE BOBBLE (MB)

TOP OF HEAD

Row 6: 1 ch, (3 dc with B, 1 dc with C) twice, (1 dc with B, 1 dc with C) twice, (1 dc with C, 1 dc with B) twice, (1 dc with C, 3 dc with B) twice, turn.

Continue on these 24 sts.

Row 7: 1 ch, 1 dc in next 5 dc with B, 1 dc with C, 1 dc in next 3 dc with B, (1 dc with C, 1 dc with B, 1 dc with C) twice, 1 dc in next 3 dc with B, 1 dc with C, 1 dc in next 5 dc with B, turn.

Row 8: 1 ch, *1 dc in next 4 dc with B, 1 dc in next with C, 1 dc in next 4 dc with B*, 1 dc in next 6 dc with C; rep from * to *, turn.

Row 9: 1 ch, 1 dc in next 3 dc with B, 1 dc in next with C, 1 dc in next 7 dc with B, 1 dc in next 2 dc with C, 1 dc in next 7 dc with B, 1 dc in next with C, 1 dc in next 3 dc with B, turn.

Row 10: 1 ch, 1 dc in next 2 dc with B, 1 dc in next with C, 1 dc in next 8 dc with B, 1 dc in next 2 dc with C, 1 dc in next 8 dc with B, 1 dc in next with C, 1 dc in next 2 dc with B, turn.

Row 11 (dec): 1 ch, (1 dc, dc2tog, 1 dc) twice with C, 1 dc in next dc with B, dc2tog with C, 1 dc in next 2 dc with B, dc2tog with C, 1 dc in next dc with B, (1 dc, dc2tog, 1 dc) twice with C, turn (18 sts).

Row 12 (dec): 1 ch, *dc2tog with C; with B, 1 dc in next dc, dc2tog, 1 dc in next dc; dc2tog with C*, 1 dc in next 2 dc with B; rep from * to *, turn (12 sts).

Row 13 (dec): 1 ch, (dc2tog) twice with C, (dc2tog) twice with B, (dc2tog) twice with C (6 sts).

Fasten off and thread C through last 6 stitches. Pull tightly on end of yarn and fasten off.

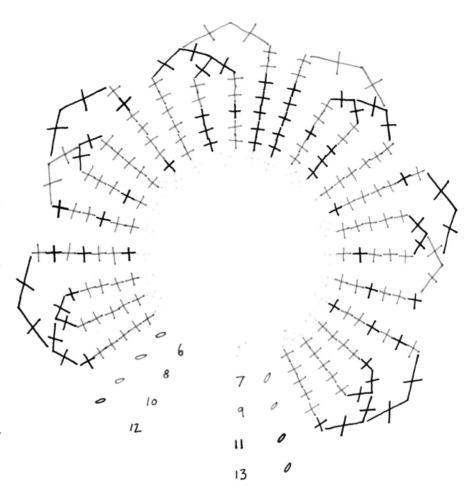

TOP OF HEAD
ROWS 6–13

COLOUR KEY FOR YARNS

FOR SHAPE FACE, TOP OF HEAD, NECK, SHAPE MIDDLE OF BODY, FRONT LEGS: SHAPE LEGS, HIND LEGS: SHAPE LEG AND RIGHT THIGH, TAIL: STRIPES

All other charts are shown in alternate rounds/rows of blue and black.

NECK

With RS of head facing, 3.25mm hook and A, sl st to first of unworked 6 dc of row 4 of shape face.

Row 1 (RS): 1 dc in same st as sl st, 1 dc in next 5 dc. Join B in last dc and work 7 dc evenly along edge of the 8 rows of the first side of the head, joining C in the sixth st and working last dc with C; work 7 dc evenly along edge of the 8 rows of the other side of the head, changing to B for the last 6 dc, sl st to first dc with C, turn (20 sts).

Row 2 (WS): 1 dc in next 5 dc with C, 1 dc in next dc with B, 1 dc in next 2 dc with C, 1 dc in next dc with B, 1 dc in next 11 dc with C, turn.

Row 3 (inc): With A, 1 ch, (1 dc, dc2inc, 1 dc) twice; with B, 1 dc in next dc, dc2inc, 1 dc in next 4 dc; 1 dc in next 2 dc with C; with B work 1 dc in next 4 dc, dc2inc, 1 dc in next dc, sl st to first dc, turn (24 sts).

Row 4: 1 dc in next 7 dc with B, 1 dc in next 2 dc with C, 1 dc in next 7 dc with B, 1 dc in next 8 dc with A, turn.

Row 5: 1 ch, 1 dc in next 8 dc with A, 1 dc in next 6 dc with C, 1 dc in next dc with B, 1 dc in next 2 dc with C, 1 dc in next dc with B, 1 dc in next 6 dc with C, do not turn.

Next: 1 dc in next 8 dc with C. Sl st to next st and fasten off, leaving a long tail of C.

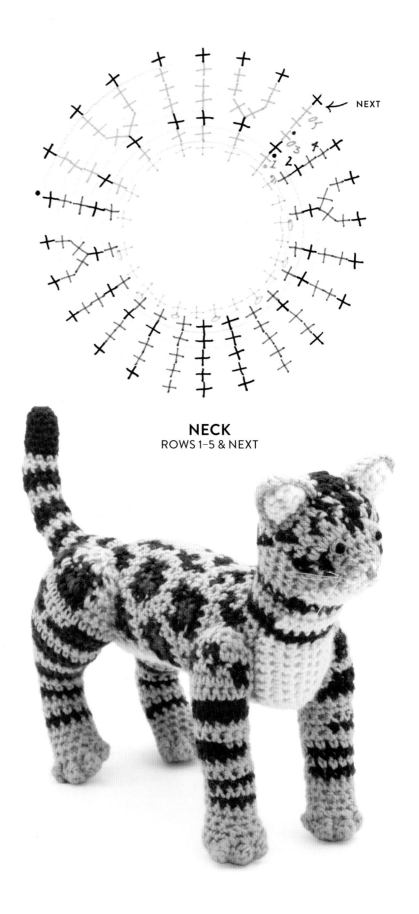

NECK
ROWS 1–5 & NEXT

NEXT

Ears (make 2)

With 3.25mm hook and A, make 4 ch.
Row 1: 1 dc in 2nd ch from hook, 1 dc in next ch, 3 dc in next ch, 1 dc in reverse side of next 2 ch, turn (7 sts).
Row 2 (inc): 1 ch, dc2inc, 1 dc in next 2 dc, dc3inc, 1 dc in next 2 dc, dc2inc (11 sts).
Fasten off, leaving a long tail of yarn. This completes the inner ear.
With B, make one more piece to match the first for the outer ear. Turn work at the end and do not fasten off.

Body

SHAPE FRONT

Starting at front of body, with 3.25mm hook and A, make 10 ch.
Row 1 (RS): 1 dc in 2nd ch from hook, 1 dc in next 7 ch, 2 dc in end ch, 1 dc in reverse side of next 8 ch, turn (18 sts).
Row 2 (WS) (inc): 1 ch, (dc2inc, 2 dc) 6 times, sl st to first dc, turn (24 sts).
Row 3 (inc): (Dc2inc, 3 dc) 6 times, turn (30 sts).
Row 4: 1 ch, 1 dc in each dc, sl st to first dc, turn.

JOIN EAR PIECES

Place the two ear pieces together, with the inner ear facing up.
Next: 1 ch, inserting the hook under both loops of each stitch of the inner ear first, then the outer ear at the same time to join, dc2inc, 1 dc in next 4 dc, dc3inc, 1 dc in next 4 dc, dc2inc (15 sts). Fasten off, leaving a long tail of yarn.

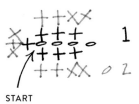

START

EARS
ROWS 1-2

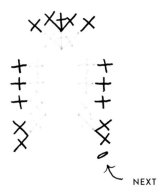

NEXT

JOIN EAR PIECES
INSERT HOOK INTO EACH STITCH OF BOTH EAR PIECES AT SAME TIME TO JOIN

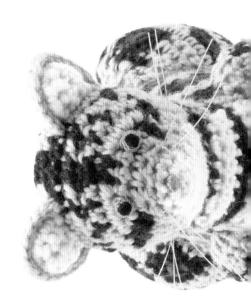

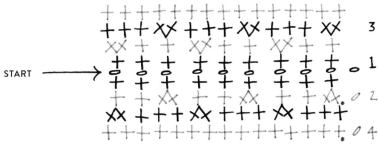

START

SHAPE FRONT
ROWS 1-4

SHAPE MIDDLE OF BODY

Row 1 (RS): 1 dc in next 3 dc. Join B in last dc and carry unused yarn on WS of work. With B, work 1 dc in next 24 dc, turn, finishing 3 sts before the end of the row.

Row 2 (WS): 1 ch, 1 dc in next 24 dc with B, 1 dc in next 6 dc with A, sl st to first dc, turn.

Row 3: 1 dc in next 6 dc with A, 1 dc in next 24 dc with B, turn.

Row 4: 1 ch, 1 dc in next 6 dc. Join C in last dc and carry unused yarn on WS of work. 1 dc in next 2 dc with C, 1 dc in next 8 dc with B, 1 dc in next 2 dc with C, 1 dc in next 6 dc with B,

1 dc in next 6 dc with A, sl st to first dc, turn.

Row 5: 1 dc in next 6 dc with A, 1 dc in next 6 dc with B, (2 dc with C, 3 dc with B) twice, 1 dc in next 2 dc with C, 1 dc in next 6 dc with B, turn.

Row 6: 1 ch, 1 dc in next 7 dc with B, (2 dc with C, 2 dc with B) twice, 1 dc in next 2 dc with C, 1 dc in next 7 dc with B, 1 dc in next 6 dc with A, sl st to first dc, turn.

Row 7: 1 dc in next 6 dc with A, 1 dc in next 10 dc with B, 1 dc in next 4 dc with C, 1 dc in next 10 dc with B, turn.

Row 8: 1 ch, 1 dc in next 10 dc with B, 1 dc in next dc with C, 1 dc in next 2 dc with B, 1 dc in next dc with C, 1 dc in next 10 dc with B, 1 dc in next 6 dc with A, sl st to first dc, turn.

Row 9: 1 dc in next 6 dc with A, 1 dc in next 2 dc with C, 1 dc in next 2 dc with B, 1 dc in next 4 dc with C, 1 dc in next dc with B, 1 dc in next 2 dc with C, 1 dc in next 2 dc with B, 1 dc in next 2 dc with C, 1 dc in next dc with B, 1 dc in next 4 dc with C, 1 dc in next 2 dc with B, 1 dc in next 2 dc with C, turn.

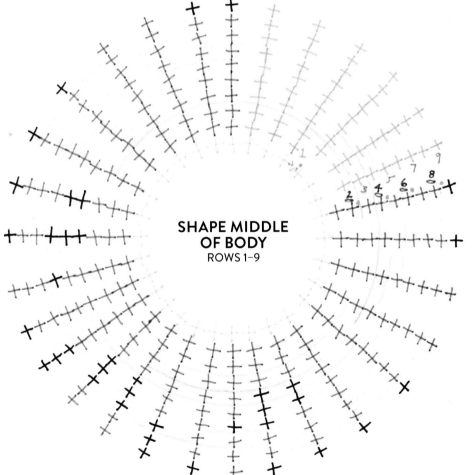

**SHAPE MIDDLE
OF BODY**
ROWS 1–9

Row 10: 1 ch, 1 dc in next 2 dc with C, 1 dc in next 2 dc with B, 1 dc in next dc with C. Join D in last dc and work 1 dc in next 2 dc with D, 1 dc in next dc with C, 1 dc in next 8 dc with B, 1 dc in next dc with C, 1 dc in next 2 dc with D, 1 dc in next dc with C, 1 dc in next 2 dc with B, 1 dc in next 2 dc with C, 1 dc in next 6 dc with A, sl st to first dc, turn.

Row 11: 1 dc in next 6 dc with A, 1 dc in next 4 dc with B, 1 dc in next dc with C, 1 dc in next 2 dc with D, 1 dc in next dc with C, 1 dc in next 3 dc with B, 1 dc in next 2 dc with C, 1 dc in next 3 dc with B, 1 dc in next dc with C, 1 dc in next 2 dc with D, 1 dc in next dc with C, 1 dc in next 4 dc with B, turn.

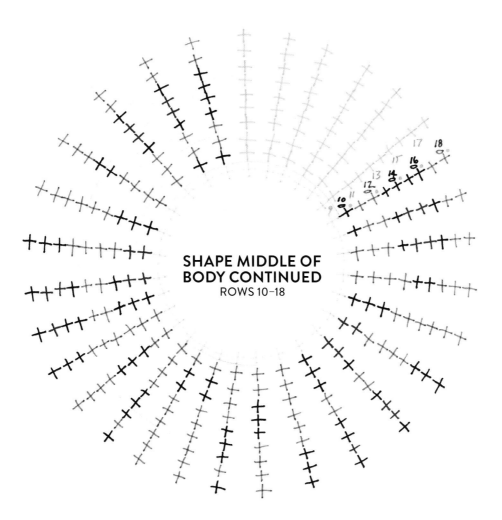

SHAPE MIDDLE OF BODY CONTINUED
ROWS 10–18

Row 12: 1 ch, 1 dc in next 4 dc with B, (1 dc with C, 1 dc with B, 2 dc with C, 1 dc with B) 3 times, 1 dc in next dc with C, 1 dc in next 4 dc with B, 1 dc in next 6 dc with A, sl st to first dc, turn.

Row 13: 1 dc in next 6 dc with A, 1 dc in next 3 dc with C, 1 dc in next 6 dc with B, 1 dc in next dc with C, 1 dc in next 4 dc with B, 1 dc in next dc with C, 1 dc in next 6 dc with B, 1 dc in next 3 dc with C, turn.

Row 14: 1 ch, 1 dc in next dc with C, 1 dc in next 2 dc with D, 1 dc in next dc with C, 1 dc in next 5 dc with B, 1 dc in next 2 dc with C, 1 dc in next 2 dc with B, 1 dc in next 2 dc with C, 1 dc in next 5 dc with B, 1 dc in next dc with C, 1 dc in next 2 dc with D, 1

dc in next dc with C, 1 dc in next 6 dc with A, sl st to first dc, turn.

Row 15: 1 dc in next 6 dc with A, 1 dc in next dc with C, 1 dc in next 2 dc with D, *1 dc in next dc with C, 1 dc in next 2 dc with B, 1 dc in next 2 dc with C, 1 dc in next 2 dc with B, 1 dc in next dc with C*, 1 dc in next 2 dc with B; rep from * to *, 1 dc in next 2 dc with D, 1 dc in next dc with C, turn.

Row 16: 1 ch, 1 dc in next 3 dc with C, 1 dc in next 2 dc with B, 1 dc in next dc with C, 1 dc in next dc with D, 1 dc in next 2 dc with C, (1 dc with B, 1 dc with C, 1 dc with B) twice, 1 dc in next 2 dc with C, 1 dc in next dc with D, 1 dc in next dc with C, 1 dc in next 2 dc with B, 1 dc in next 3 dc with C,

1 dc in next 6 dc with A, sl st to first dc, turn.

Row 17: 1 dc in next 6 dc with A, 1 dc in next 5 dc with B, 1 dc in next dc with C, 1 dc in next 2 dc with D, 1 dc in next dc with C, 1 dc in next 6 dc with B, 1 dc in next dc with C, 1 dc in next 2 dc with D, 1 dc in next dc with C, 1 dc in next 5 dc with B, turn.

Row 18: 1 ch, 1 dc in next 5 dc with B, 1 dc in next 4 dc with C, (1 dc with B, 1 dc with C, 1 dc with B) twice, 1 dc in next 4 dc with C, 1 dc in next 5 dc with B, 1 dc in next 6 dc with A, sl st to first dc, turn.

Row 19: 1 dc in next 6 dc with A, 1 dc in next dc with B, 1 dc in next dc with C, 1 dc in next 2 dc with D, 1 dc in next 6 dc with B, 1 dc in next dc with C, 1 dc in next 2 dc with B, 1 dc in next dc with C, 1 dc in next 6 dc with B, 1 dc in next 2 dc with D, 1 dc in next dc with C, 1 dc in next dc with B, turn.

Row 20: 1 ch, 1 dc in next dc with B, 1 dc in next 4 dc with C, 1 dc in next 5 dc with B, 1 dc in next dc with C, 1 dc in next 2 dc with B, 1 dc in next dc with C, 1 dc in next 5 dc with B, 1 dc in next 4 dc with C, 1 dc in next dc with B, 1 dc in next 6 dc with A, sl st to first dc, turn.

Row 21: 1 dc in next 6 dc with A, 1 dc in next 7 dc with B, 1 dc in next 2 dc with C, (1 dc with B, 1 dc with C, 1 dc with B) twice, 1 dc in next 2 dc with C, 1 dc in next 7 dc with B, turn.

Row 22: 1 ch, 1 dc in next 7 dc with B, 1 dc in next 2 dc with C, 1 dc in next 6 dc with B, 1 dc in next 2 dc with C, 1 dc in next 7 dc with B, 1 dc in next 6 dc with A, sl st to first dc, turn.

Row 23: 1 dc in next 6 dc with A, 1 dc in next 8 dc with B, 1 dc in next 2 dc with C, (1 dc with B, 2 dc with C) twice, 1 dc in next 8 dc with B, turn.

Row 24: 1 ch, 1 dc in next 8 dc with B, (2 dc with C, 1 dc with B) twice, 1 dc in next 2 dc with C, 1 dc in next 8 dc with B, 1 dc in next 6 dc with A, sl st to first dc, turn.

Rows 25–26: Rep rows 23–24.

Row 27: 1 dc in next 6 dc with A, 1 dc in next 11 dc with B, 1 dc in next 2 dc with C, 1 dc in next 11 dc with B, do not turn.

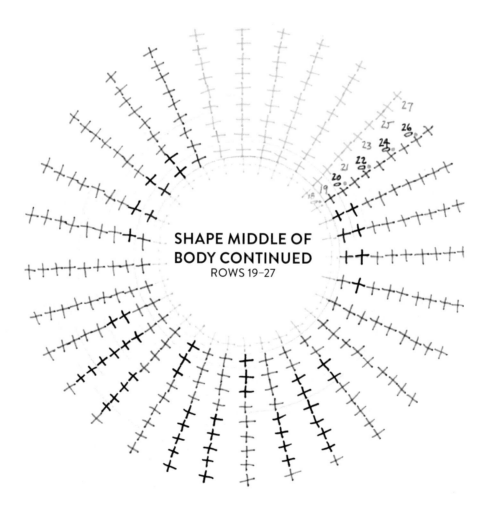

SHAPE MIDDLE OF BODY CONTINUED
ROWS 19–27

SHAPE END OF BODY

The following is worked in rounds.
Continue with B.

Round 1 (dec): (Dc2tog, 3 dc) 6 times
(24 sts).

Stuff body before continuing.

Round 2 (dec): (Dc2tog, 2 dc) 6 times
(18 sts).

Round 3 (dec): (Dc2tog, 1 dc) 6 times
(12 sts).

Round 4 (dec): (Dc2tog) 6 times
(6 sts).

Break yarn and thread through last
6 stitches. Pull tightly on end of yarn
to close. Fasten off.

Front legs (make 2)

RIGHT PAW

The bobbles appear on the reverse
side of the work. This will be the right
side. See page 166 for instructions to
make bobble (mb).

Starting at the base of the paw,
with 3.25mm hook and B, make a
magic loop.

Round 1 (WS): 1 ch, 6 dc into loop
(6 sts).

Round 2 (inc): (Dc2inc) 6 times
(12 sts). Pull tightly on short end of
yarn to close loop.

Round 3 (inc): (Dc2inc, 2 dc) 4 times
(16 sts).

Round 4: 1 dc in next 8 dc, (mb, 1 dc
in next dc) 4 times, turn.

RIGHT LEG

The following is worked in rows.

Row 1 (RS) (dec): 1 ch, 1 dc in first
dc, (1 dc in next st, dc2tog) twice,
1 dc in next 9 dc, turn (14 sts).

Row 2 (WS) (dec): 1 ch, 1 dc in next
8 dc, (dc2tog, 1 dc in next dc) twice,
turn (12 sts).

Rows 3–4: 1 ch, 1 dc in each dc, turn.
Join C in last dc and carry unused
yarn on WS of work.

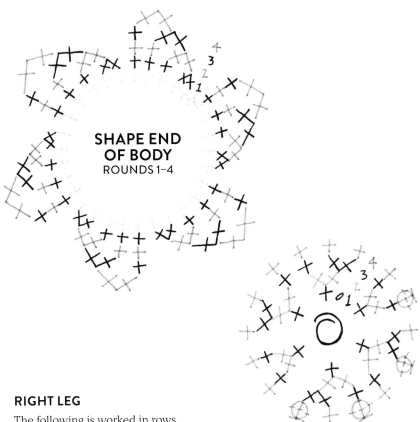

**SHAPE END
OF BODY**
ROUNDS 1–4

FRONT LEGS
RIGHT PAW
ROUNDS 1–4

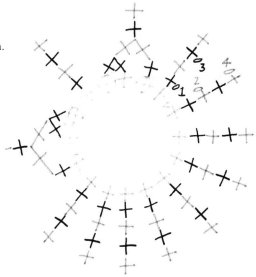

FRONT LEGS CONTINUED
RIGHT LEG
ROUNDS 1–4

SHAPE LEG

Row 5: 1 ch, 1 dc in next 6 dc with C, 1 dc in next 6 dc with B, turn.

Row 6: 1 ch, 1 dc in each dc with B, turn.

Row 7: Rep round 5.

Rows 8–9: 1 ch, 1 dc in each dc with B, turn.

Row 10: 1 ch, 1 dc in next 2 dc with B, 1 dc in next 8 dc with C, 1 dc in next 2 dc with B, turn.

Row 11: 1 ch, 1 dc in next 4 dc with B, 1 dc in next 4 dc with C, 1 dc in next 4 dc with B, turn.

Rows 12–13: 1 ch, 1 dc in each dc with B, turn.

Row 14 (inc): 1 ch, 1 dc in next 3 dc with B; with C, (dc2inc, 3 dc) twice, dc2inc, turn (15 sts).

Row 15: 1 ch, 1 dc in next 3 dc with B, 1 dc in next 7 dc with C, 1 dc in next 5 dc with B, turn.

Row 16 (inc): 1 ch, (dc2inc, 4 dc) 3 times with B, turn (18 sts).

Row 17: 1 ch, 1 dc in next 4 dc with B, 1 dc in next 2 dc with C, 1 dc in next 12 dc with B, turn.

Row 18: 1 ch, 1 dc in next 5 dc with B, 1 dc in next 2 dc with C, 1 dc in next 2 dc with B, 1 dc in next dc with C, 1 dc in next dc with B, 1 dc in next 2 dc with C, 1 dc in next 5 dc with B, turn.

Row 19: 1 ch, 1 dc in next 8 dc with B, 1 dc in next 2 dc with C, 1 dc in next dc with B, 1 dc in next 3 dc with C, 1 dc in next 4 dc with B, turn. Continue with B.

Row 20 (dec): 1 ch, (dc2tog, 1 dc) 6 times, turn (12 sts).

Row 21 (dec): 1 ch, (dc2tog) 6 times (6 sts).

Fasten off, leaving a long tail of B at the end.

LEFT PAW

Starting at the base of the paw, with 3.25mm hook and B, make a magic loop.

Rounds 1–3: Work as for rounds 1–3 of right front paw.

Round 4: (1 dc, mb) 4 times, 1 dc in next 8 dc. Do not turn.

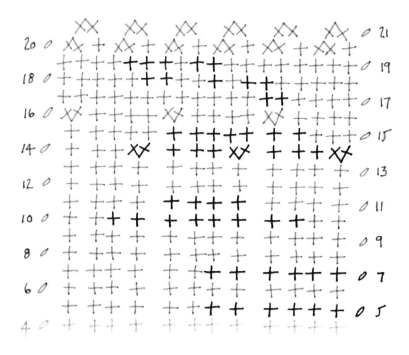

FRONT LEGS CONTINUED
SHAPE LEG
ROWS 5–21

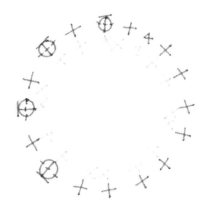

FRONT LEGS CONTINUED
LEFT PAW
ROUND 4

LEFT LEG

The following is worked in rows.

Row 1 (WS) (dec): 1 dc in next dc, (1 dc in next st, dc2tog) twice, 1 dc in next 9 dc, turn.

Row 2 (RS) (dec): 1 ch, 1 dc in next 8 dc, (dc2tog, 1 dc in next dc) twice, turn (12 sts).

Rows 3–4: Work as for rows 3–21 of right leg.

SHAPE LEG

Rows 5–21: Work as for rows 5–21 of right leg.

Fasten off, leaving a long tail of B at the end.

Hind legs

RIGHT PAW

Starting at the base of the paw, with 3.25mm hook and B, make a magic loop.

Rounds 1–4 (WS): Work as for rounds 1–4 of right front paw.

Round 5 (RS) (dec): 1 ch, 1 dc in first dc, (1 dc in next st, dc2tog) twice, 1 dc in next 9 dc (14 sts).

Round 6 (dec): (1 dc in next dc, dc2tog) twice, 1 dc in next 8 dc (12 sts).

Rounds 7–8: 1 dc in each dc.

Join C in last dc and carry unused yarn on WS of work.

SHAPE LEG

Round 9: 1 dc in next 6 dc with C, 1 dc in next 6 dc with B.

Rounds 10–11: 1 dc in each dc with B.

Round 12: 1 dc in next dc with B, 1 dc in next 6 dc with C, 1 dc in next 5 dc with B.

FRONT LEGS CONTINUED
LEFT LEG
ROWS 1–2

HIND LEGS
RIGHT PAW
ROUNDS 5–8

HIND LEGS CONTINUED
SHAPE LEG
ROUNDS 9–12

SHAPE BACK OF LEG

Continue with B.

Round 13: 1 dc in next dc, ending at the side of the leg; 6 ch, skip the 6 dc at the front of the leg, 1 dc in next 5 dc.

Round 14: 1 dc in next dc, 1 dc in next 6 ch, 1 dc in next 5 dc. Break yarn and thread through last round of stitches. Pull tightly on end of yarn to close and fasten off.

SHAPE RIGHT THIGH

With RS of leg facing, 3.25mm hook, join B with a sl st to first of 6 skipped dc of round 12.

Row 1 (RS): 1 dc in same st as sl st, 1 dc in next 5 dc, 1 dc in reverse side of next 6 ch, turn (12 sts).

Row 2 (WS): 1 ch, 1 dc in each dc, turn. Join C in last dc and carry unused yarn on WS of work.

Row 3 (inc): With C, 1 ch, (dc2inc, 1 dc) 6 times, turn (18 sts).

Row 4: 1 ch, 1 dc in next 9 dc with B, 1 dc in next 9 dc with C, turn.

Rows 5–6: 1 ch, 1 dc in each dc with B, turn.

Row 7 (inc): 1 ch, (2 dc, dc2inc) 6 times with C, turn (24 sts).

Row 8: 1 ch, 1 dc in each dc with C, turn.

Row 9: 1 ch, 1 dc in each dc with B, turn.

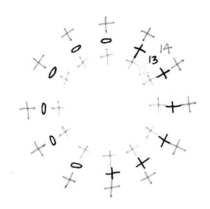

HIND LEGS CONTINUED
SHAPE BACK OF LEG
ROUNDS 13–14

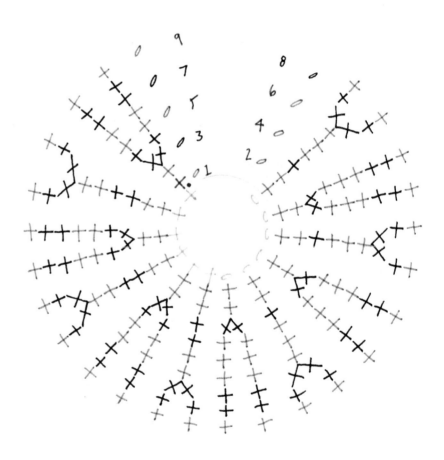

HIND LEGS CONTINUED
SHAPE RIGHT THIGH
ROWS 1–9

Row 10: 1 ch, 1 dc in next 7 dc with B, 1 dc in next 2 dc with C, join D in last dc and work 1 dc in next 2 dc with D, 1 dc in next 13 dc with B, turn.

Row 11 (inc): With C, 1 ch, (dc2inc, 3 dc) twice, dc2inc, 1 dc in next 2 dc; 1 dc in next dc with B, dc2inc with C, 1 dc in next 2 dc with D; with C, 1 dc in next dc, dc2inc; with B, 1 dc in next 3 dc, dc2inc, 1 dc in next 3 dc, turn (30 sts).

Row 12: 1 ch, 1 dc in next 11 dc with B, 1 dc in next 2 dc with C, 1 dc in

next 5 dc with B, 1 dc in next 12 dc with C, turn.

Row 13: 1 ch, 1 dc in next 20 dc with B, 1 dc in next 2 dc with C, 1 dc in next 8 dc with B, turn.

Row 14: 1 ch, 1 dc in next 8 dc with B, 1 dc in next dc with C, 1 dc in next 2 dc with D, 1 dc in next dc with C, 1 dc in next dc with B, 1 dc in next 5 dc with C, 1 dc in next 12 dc with B, turn.

Row 15 (dec): With B, 1 ch, (3 dc, dc2tog) twice, 1 dc in next 2 dc; 1 dc

in next dc with C; with D, dc2tog, 1 dc in next dc; with C, 1 dc in next dc; 1 dc in next dc with B; with C, dc2tog, 1 dc in next 2 dc; with B, 1 dc in next dc, dc2tog, 1 dc in next 3 dc, dc2tog, turn (24 sts).

Row 16 (dec): With B, 1 ch, (2 dc, dc2tog) twice, 1 dc in next 2 dc; with C, dc2tog, 1 dc in next 2 dc; (dc2tog, 2 dc) twice with B, dc2tog, turn (18 sts).

Continue with B.

Row 17 (dec): 1 ch, (1 dc, dc2tog) 6 times (12 sts).

Row 18 (dec): (Dc2tog) 6 times (6 sts). Fasten off, leaving a long tail of B at the end.

LEFT PAW

Starting at the base of the paw, with 3.25mm hook and B, make a magic loop.

Rounds 1–14: Work as for rounds 1–14 of right hind leg.

SHAPE LEFT THIGH

Follow charts for right thigh.

With WS of leg facing, 3.25mm hook, join B with a sl st to first of 6 skipped dc of round 12.

Row 1 (WS): 1 dc in same st as sl st, 1 dc in next 5 dc, 1 dc in reverse side of next 6 ch, turn (12 sts).

Row 2 (RS): 1 ch, 1 dc in each dc, turn. Join C in last dc and carry unused yarn on WS of work.

Rows 3–18: Work as for rows 3–18 of right thigh.

Fasten off, leaving a long tail of B at the end.

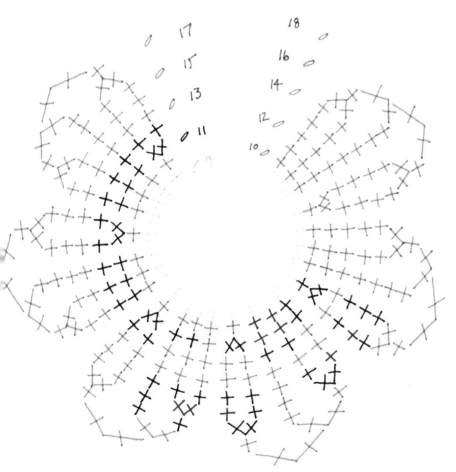

HIND LEGS CONTINUED
SHAPE RIGHT THIGH
ROWS 10–18

Tail

TIP

With 3.25mm hook and C, make a magic loop.

Round 1: 1 ch, 6 dc into loop (6 sts).

Round 2 (inc): (Dc2inc, 1 dc) 3 times (9 sts). Pull tightly on short end of yarn to close loop.

Rounds 3–7: 1 dc in each dc. Join B in last dc and carry unused yarn on WS of work.

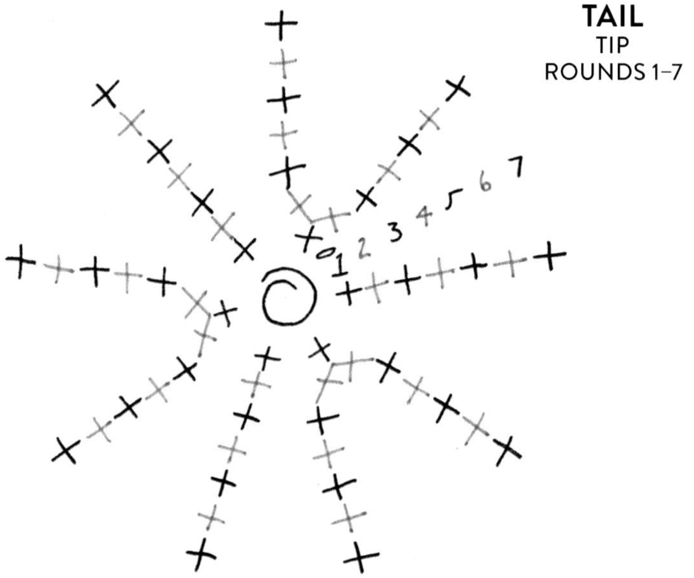

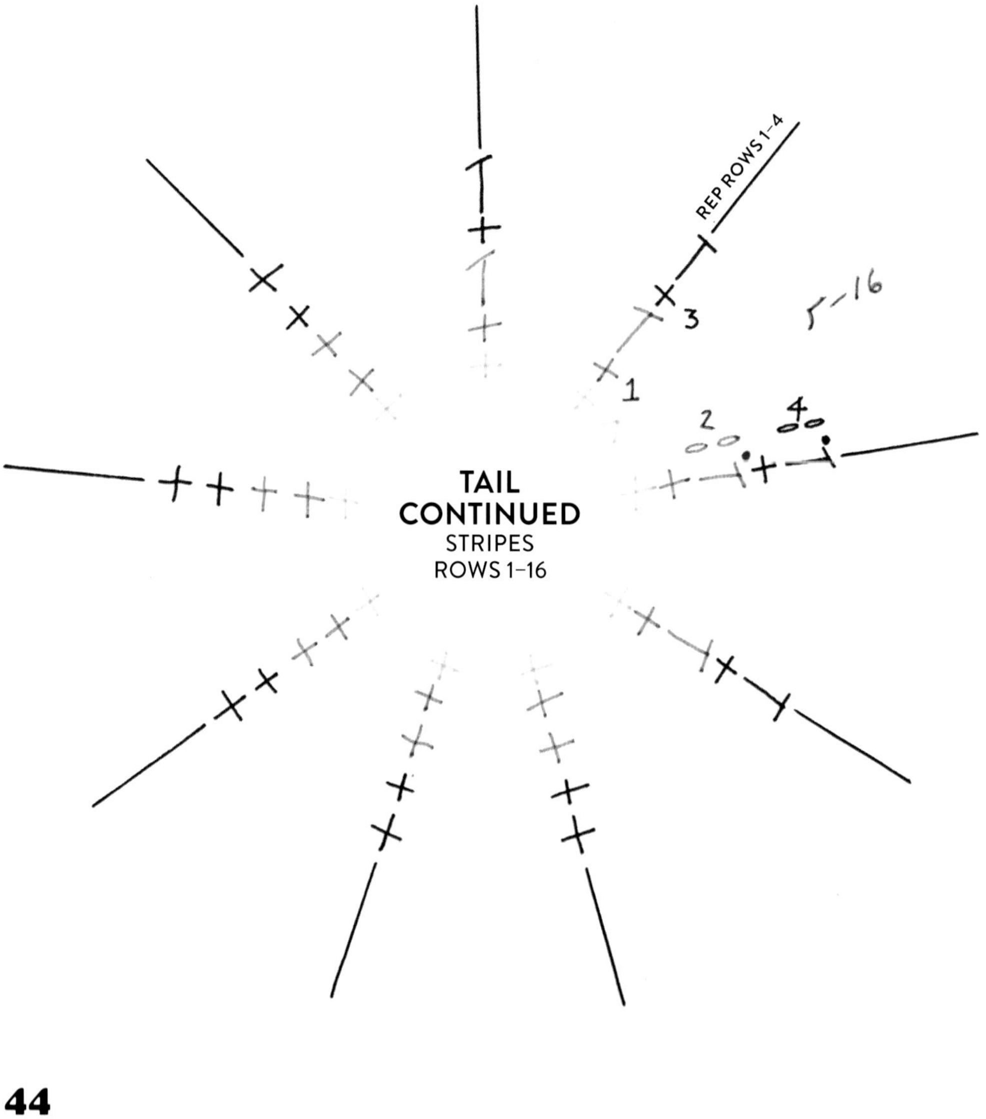

TAIL
TIP
ROUNDS 1–7

0 1 2 3 4 5 6 7

REP ROWS 1-4

5-16

3

1

2   4

TAIL CONTINUED
STRIPES
ROWS 1–16

STRIPES

The following is worked in rows.

Row 1 (RS): 1 dc in each st with B, turn.

Row 2 (WS): 2 ch, 1 htr in next 2 dc, 1 dc in next 5 dc, 1 htr in next 2 dc, sl st to first htr, turn.

Rows 3–4: Rep rows 1–2 with C, turn.

Rows 5–16: Rep rows 1–4 3 times.

Row 17: Rep row 1.

Row 18: 1 ch, 1 dc in each dc with B, sl st to first dc, turn.

Rows 19–20: Rep rows 17–18 with C.

Rows 21–22: Rep rows 17–18 with B.

Fasten off, leaving a long tail of B.

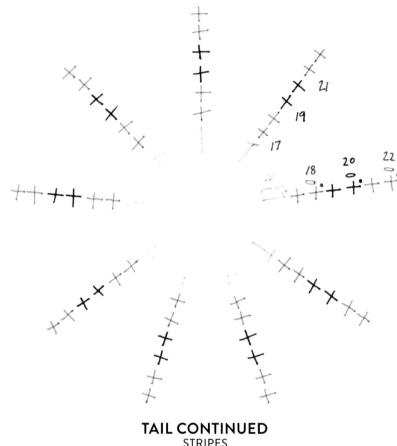

TAIL CONTINUED
STRIPES
ROWS 17–22

Making up

HEAD

Stuff the head. With the tail of yarn left after fastening off, sew the head in place. Stitch all around the neck edges. Insert more stuffing into the neck if necessary. Embroider the nose in satin stitch (see page 170) using three strands of embroidery thread. Embroider the pupils of the eyes in satin stitch and work straight stitches around the pupils to form the irises (see page 170).

EARS

Stuff the ears lightly, keeping them flat. Sew the ears in place, near the back of the head, stitching all around the lower edges with the tails of yarn left after fastening off.

LEGS

Thread tail of yarn through last row of stitches. Pull tightly on end of yarn to close. Sew the edges of the leg together, matching the rows, stuffing the leg as you sew. Flatten the top of each leg, positioning the seam down the centre of the inside leg, which will be placed against the body. Sew the legs to the body, stitching all around the top of the thighs with the tail of yarn left after fastening off.

TAIL

Stuff the tail. Sew the tail in place with the tail of yarn left after fastening off, positioning the joined edges of the rows at the back.

WHISKERS (OPTIONAL)

Attach three whiskers to the posts of the stitches on each side of the muzzle (see page 171). Trim the ends.

Weave in all the yarn ends.

Maine Coon

THE MAINE COON IS BIGGER THAN THE AVERAGE CAT, SO THIS IS A LARGER
PROJECT. VARIEGATED YARN IS USED TO CREATE THE TICKED TABBY COAT.

Materials

- Scheepjes Spirit, 56% cotton, 44% acrylic
  (230yd/210m per 50g ball), or any DK yarn:
  1 x 50g ball in 302 Wolf (A)
  2 x 50g balls in 305 Gazelle (B)
- Stranded embroidery thread in green, such as
  Anchor Stranded Cotton, shade 0266, for the eyes
- Stranded embroidery thread in black, such as
  Anchor Stranded Cotton, shade 0403, for the
  pupils
- Stranded embroidery thread in grey, such as
  Anchor Stranded Cotton, shade 0397, for the
  fluffy inner ears
- 6 lengths of 0.3mm clear nylon thread, each
  measuring 7in (18cm), for the optional whiskers
  (not suitable for young children)
- 3.25mm (UK10:USD/3) crochet hook
- Blunt-ended yarn needle
- Toy stuffing

Size

- Approximately $10^5/_8$in (27cm) body length, from
  tip of nose to back of hind legs
- Approximately 9in (23cm) tall from top of head
  (excluding ears)

Tension

25 sts and 25 rows to 4in (10cm) over double crochet
using 3.25mm hook. Use a larger or smaller hook if
necessary to obtain the correct tension.

Method

The cat's head, body and legs are worked in rounds and rows of double crochet. The first row of the muzzle is crocheted into the front loops of the previous row, and the shaping is formed by a combination of double crochet, half treble and treble stitches. The unworked back loops are crocheted to begin the rest of the head shaping. The neck is crocheted in rounds, working from the stitches at the underside of the muzzle, and then along the edges of the rows that make up the top of the head. The ears are worked in rows. Each ear is made up of two crocheted parts that are joined by crocheting into each stitch of both pieces at the same time. Loop stitch is used to form the fluffy areas of the cat's coat. A ruff is crocheted separately, slipped over the cat's head and stitched in place. The tail is crocheted in rows. A curve in the tail is formed by decreasing stitches in the last few rows. The long edges are sewn together and the tail is lightly stuffed before sewing it in place. The legs are worked in continuous rounds and rows of double crochet. The toes on the paws are produced by crocheting bobbles. The bobbles on the paws appear on the reverse side of the fabric, so the work is turned after crocheting the toes, and the paws are continued on the right side. The thighs of the hind legs are worked in rows of double crochet and loop stitch. Lengths of yarn are threaded through the stitches around the face, near the edges of the ruff. The same method is used to create the tufts of fur between the toes and on the tips of the ears. Embroidery thread is used for the finer tufts of fur on the ears. The eyes and nose are embroidered with embroidery threads and yarn.

1 ch and 2 ch at beg of the row/round does not count as a st throughout.

Muzzle

With 3.25mm hook and A, make a magic loop (see page 163).
Round 1: 1 ch, 6 dc into loop (6 sts).
Round 2 (inc): (Dc2inc) 6 times (12 sts). Pull tightly on short end of yarn to close loop.
Round 3 (inc): (Dc2inc, 1 dc) 6 times (18 sts).
Round 4 (inc): (Dc2inc, 2 dc) 6 times (24 sts).

SHAPE FRONT OF MUZZLE

Row 1: 1 dc in front loop only of next 16 sts, turn.
Row 2: Skip first dc, (1 dc in next dc, 1 htr in next dc, 1 tr in next 3 dc, 1 htr in next dc, 1 dc in next dc) twice. Join B in last dc and carry unused yarn on WS of work, sl st to next dc with B, turn.

COLOUR KEY FOR YARNS

FOR SHAPE FACE, SHAPE MIDDLE OF BODY, RUFF
All other charts are shown in alternate rounds/rows of blue and black.

MUZZLE
ROUNDS 1–4

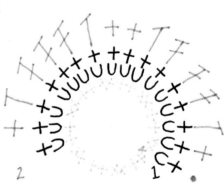

SHAPE FRONT OF MUZZLE
ROWS 1–2

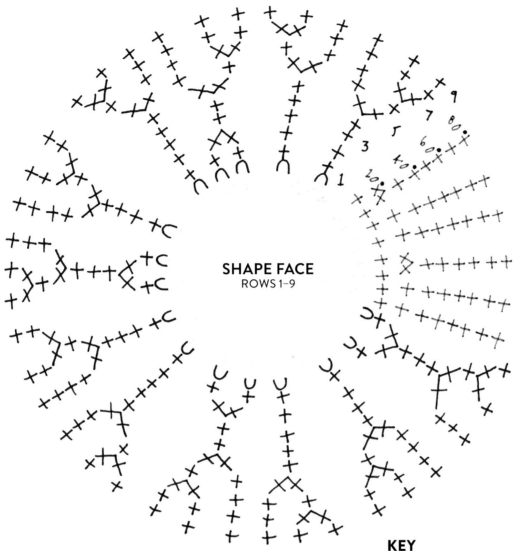

SHAPE FACE
ROWS 1–9

KEY

⟲ MAGIC LOOP

⬭ CHAIN (CH)

• SLIP STITCH (SL ST)

+ DOUBLE CROCHET (DC)

✕✕ DC2INC

✳✕ DC3INC

✕✕ DC2TOG

⊤ HALF TREBLE (HTR)

Ŧ TREBLE

⬡ MAKE LARGE BOBBLE (MLB)

ⓧ LOOP STITCH (LP ST)

SHAPE FACE

Row 1 (RS): Working in the unworked back loops of round 4 of muzzle, 1 dc in next 16 dc with B, 1 dc in both loops of next 8 dc with A, turn.

Row 2 (WS) (dec): 1 ch, (dc2tog, 2 dc) twice with A, (dc2tog, 2 dc) 4 times with B, sl st to first dc, turn (18 sts).

Row 3: 1 dc in next 12 dc with B, 1 dc in next 6 dc with A, turn.

Row 4: 1 ch, 1 dc in next 6 dc with A, 1 dc in next 12 dc with B, sl st to first dc, turn.

Row 5 (inc): (Dc2inc, 1 dc) 6 times with B, 1 dc in next 6 dc with A, turn (24 sts).

Row 6 (inc): 1 ch, 1 dc in next 6 dc with A, (dc2inc, 2 dc) 6 times with B, sl st to first dc, turn (30 sts).

Row 7 (inc): (Dc2inc, 3 dc) 6 times with B, 1 dc in next 6 dc with A, turn (36 sts).

Row 8 (inc): 1 ch, 1 dc in next 6 dc with A, (dc2inc, 4 dc) 6 times with B, sl st to first dc, turn (42 sts).

Row 9: 1 dc in next 36 dc with B, finishing 6 sts before the end, turn.

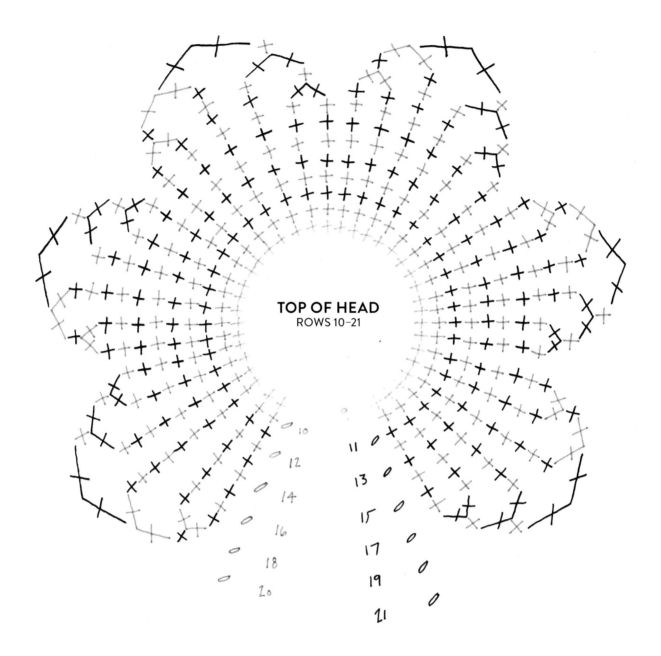

TOP OF HEAD
ROWS 10–21

TOP OF HEAD

Continue on these 36 sts with B.

Rows 10–16: 1 ch, 1 dc in each dc, turn.

Row 17 (dec): 1 ch, (dc2tog, 4 dc) 6 times, turn (30 sts).

Row 18 (dec): 1 ch, (dc2tog, 3 dc) 6 times, turn (24 sts).

Row 19 (dec): 1 ch, (dc2tog, 2 dc) 6 times, turn (18 sts).

Row 20 (dec): 1 ch, (dc2tog, 1 dc) 6 times, turn (12 sts).

Row 21 (dec): 1 ch, (dc2tog) 6 times (6 sts).

Fasten off and thread B through last 6 stitches. Pull tightly on end of yarn and fasten off.

NECK

With RS of head facing, 3.25mm hook and B, sl st to first of unworked 6 dc of row 2 of shape face.

Round 1: 1 dc in same st as sl st, 1 dc in next 5 dc, work 22 dc evenly along edge of the rows of head, turn (28 sts).

Round 2 (inc): Dc2inc, 1 dc in next 4 dc, dc2inc, (2 dc, dc2inc) 3 times, 1 dc in next 4 dc, (dc2inc, 2 dc) 3 times (36 sts).

Rounds 3–7: 1 dc in each dc.

Round 8: 1 dc in next 12 dc, sl st to next st and fasten off, leaving a long tail of yarn.

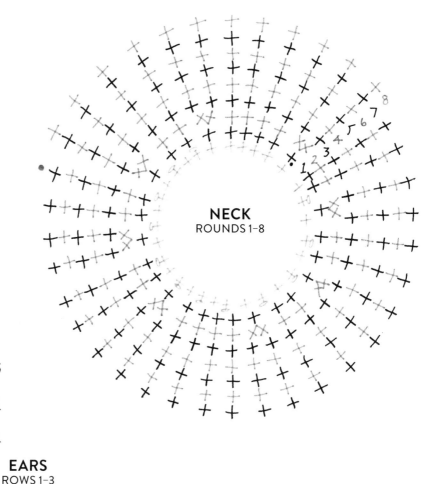

NECK
ROUNDS 1–8

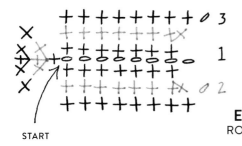

START

EARS
ROWS 1–3

Ears (make 2)

With 3.25mm hook and A, make 8 ch.

Row 1: 1 dc in 2nd ch from hook, 1 dc in next 5 ch, 3 dc in next ch, 1 dc in reverse side of next 6 ch, turn (15 sts).

Row 2 (inc): 1 ch, dc2inc, 1 dc in next 6 dc, dc3inc, 1 dc in next 6 dc, dc2inc, turn (19 sts).

Row 3: 1 ch, 1 dc in next 9 dc, dc3inc, 1 dc in next 9 dc (21 sts).

Fasten off, leaving a long tail of yarn. This completes the inner ear.

With B, make one more piece to match the first for the outer ear. Turn work at the end and do not fasten off.

JOIN EAR PIECES

Place the two ear pieces together, with the inner ear facing up.

Next: 1 ch, inserting the hook under both loops of each stitch of the inner ear first, then the outer ear at the same time to join, dc2inc, 1 dc in next 9 dc, dc3inc, 1 dc in next 9 dc, dc2inc (25 sts). Fasten off, leaving a long tail of yarn.

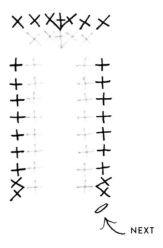

NEXT

JOIN EAR PIECES
INSERT HOOK INTO EACH
STITCH OF BOTH EAR PIECES
AT SAME TIME TO JOIN

51

Body

The loops appear on the reverse side of the work. This will be the right side. See page 166 for instructions on loop stitch (lp st).

SHAPE FRONT

Starting at front of body, with 3.25mm hook and A, make 10 ch.

Row 1 (RS): 1 dc in 2nd ch from hook, 1 dc in next 7 ch, 2 dc in end ch, 1 dc in reverse side of next 8 ch, turn (18 sts).

Row 2 (WS) (inc): 1 ch, (2 lp sts in next dc, 1 lp st in next 2 dc) 6 times, sl st to first st, turn (24 sts).

Row 3 (inc): (Dc2inc, 3 dc) 6 times, turn (30 sts).

Row 4 (inc): 1 ch, (2 lp sts in next dc, 1 lp st in next 4 dc) 6 times, sl st to first st, turn (36 sts).

Row 5 (inc): (Dc2inc, 5 dc) 6 times, turn (42 sts).

Row 6 (inc): 1 ch, (2 lp sts in next dc, 1 lp st in next 6 dc) 6 times, sl st to first st, turn (48 sts).

Row 7 (inc): (Dc2inc, 7 dc) 6 times, turn (54 sts).

Row 8: 1 ch, 1 lp st in each dc, sl st to first st, turn.

SHAPE MIDDLE OF BODY

Row 1 (RS): 1 dc in next 5 dc. Join B in last dc and carry unused yarn on WS of work. With B, work 1 dc in next 44 dc, turn, finishing 5 sts before the end of the row.

Row 2 (WS): 1 ch, 1 dc in next 44 dc with B, 1 lp st in next 10 dc with A, sl st to first dc, turn.

Row 3: 1 dc in next 10 sts with A, 1 dc in next 44 dc with B, turn.

Rows 4–25: Rep rows 2–3 11 times.

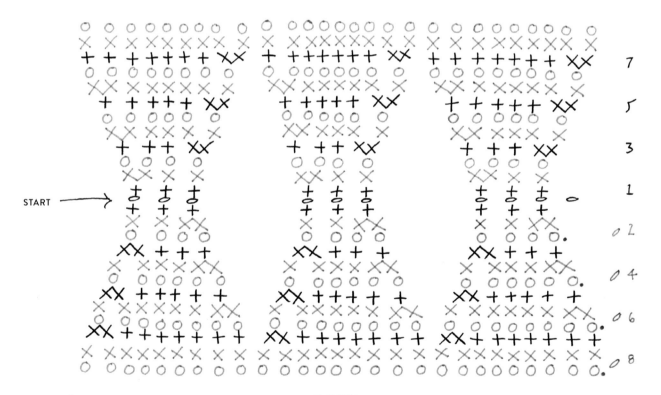

START

BODY
SHAPE FRONT
ROWS 1–8

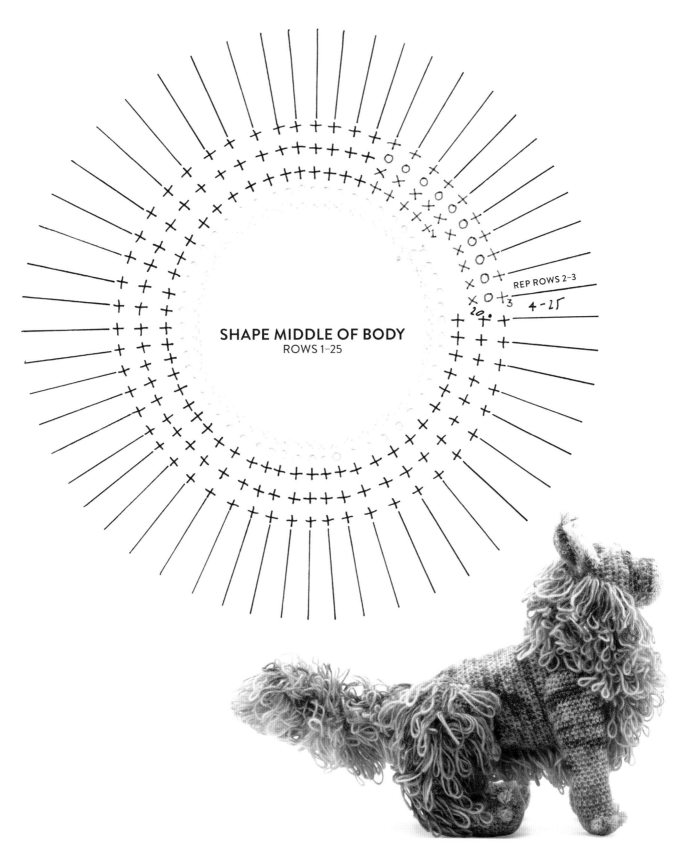

SHAPE MIDDLE OF BODY
ROWS 1–25

REP ROWS 2–3
4-25

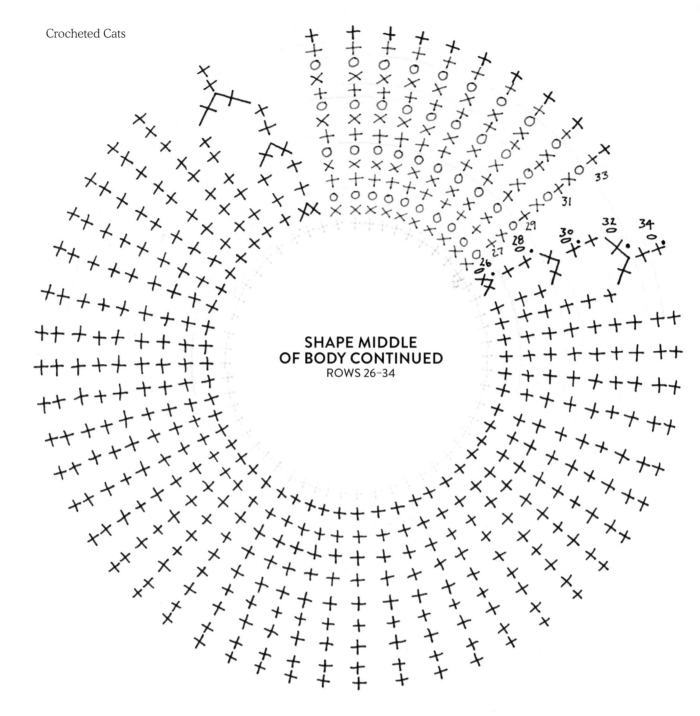

**SHAPE MIDDLE
OF BODY CONTINUED**
ROWS 26–34

Row 26 (dec): 1 ch, dc2tog, 1 dc in next 40 dc, dc2tog with B, 1 lp st in next 10 dc with A, sl st to first dc, turn (52 sts).

Row 27: 1 dc in next 10 sts with A, 1 dc in next 42 dc with B, turn.

Row 28: 1 ch, 1 dc in next 42 dc with B, 1 lp st in next 10 dc with A, sl st to first dc, turn.

Row 29 (dec): 1 dc in next 10 sts with A; with B, dc2tog, 1 dc in next 38 dc, dc2tog, turn (50 sts).

Row 30: 1 ch, 1 dc in next 40 dc with B, 1 lp st in next 10 dc with A, sl st to first dc, turn.

Row 31: 1 dc in next 10 sts with A, 1 dc in next 40 dc with B, turn.

Row 32 (dec): 1 ch, dc2tog, 1 dc in next 36 dc, dc2tog with B, 1 lp st in next 10 dc with A, sl st to first dc, turn (48 sts).

Row 33: 1 dc in next 10 dc with A, 1 dc in next 38 dc with B, turn.

Row 34: 1 ch, 1 dc in each st with B, sl st to first dc, turn.

SHAPE END OF BODY

The following is worked in rounds.
Continue with B.

Round 1 (dec): (Dc2tog, 6 dc) 6 times (42 sts).

Round 2 (dec): (Dc2tog, 5 dc) 6 times (36 sts).

Stuff body before continuing.

Round 3 (dec): (Dc2tog, 4 dc) 6 times (30 sts).

Round 4 (dec): (Dc2tog, 3 dc) 6 times (24 sts).

Round 5 (dec): (Dc2tog, 2 dc) 6 times (18 sts).

Round 6 (dec): (Dc2tog, 1 dc) 6 times (12 sts).

Round 7 (dec): (Dc2tog) 6 times (6 sts).

Break yarn and thread through last 6 stitches. Pull tightly on end of yarn to close. Fasten off.

Front legs (make 2)

The bobbles appear on the reverse side of the work. This will be the right side. See page 166 for instructions to make large bobble (mlb).

Starting at the base of the paw, with 3.25mm hook and A, make a magic loop.

Round 1 (WS): 1 ch, 6 dc into loop (6 sts).

Round 2 (inc): (Dc2inc) 6 times (12 sts). Pull tightly on short end of yarn to close loop.

Round 3 (inc): (Dc2inc, 1 dc) 6 times (18 sts).

Round 4 (inc): (Dc2inc, 2 dc) 6 times (24 sts).

Round 5: 1 dc in next 12 dc, (1 dc in next dc, mlb, 1 dc in next dc) 4 times, turn.

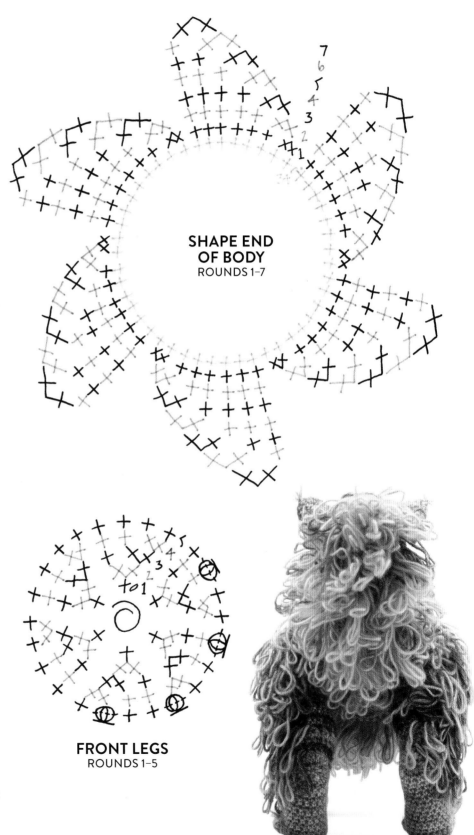

SHAPE END OF BODY
ROUNDS 1–7

FRONT LEGS
ROUNDS 1–5

55

FRONT LEGS CONTINUED
ROUNDS 6–18

Round 6 (RS) (dec): 1 ch, (dc2tog, 1 dc in next st) twice, (1 dc in next dc, dc2tog) twice, 1 dc in next 12 dc (20 sts).

Round 7 (dec): (1 dc in next st, dc2tog, 1 dc in next st) twice, 1 dc in next 12 dc (18 sts).

Rounds 8–16: 1 dc in each dc. Join B in last dc. Continue with B.

Rounds 17–18: 1 dc in each dc.

Round 19 (inc): (Dc2inc, 5 dc) 3 times (21 sts).

Rounds 20–22: 1 dc in each dc.

Round 23 (inc): (Dc2inc, 6 dc) 3 times (24 sts).

Rounds 24–26: 1 dc in each dc.

Round 27 (inc): (Dc2inc, 7 dc) 3 times (27 sts).

Rounds 28–30: 1 dc in each dc.

FRONT LEGS CONTINUED
ROUNDS 19–30

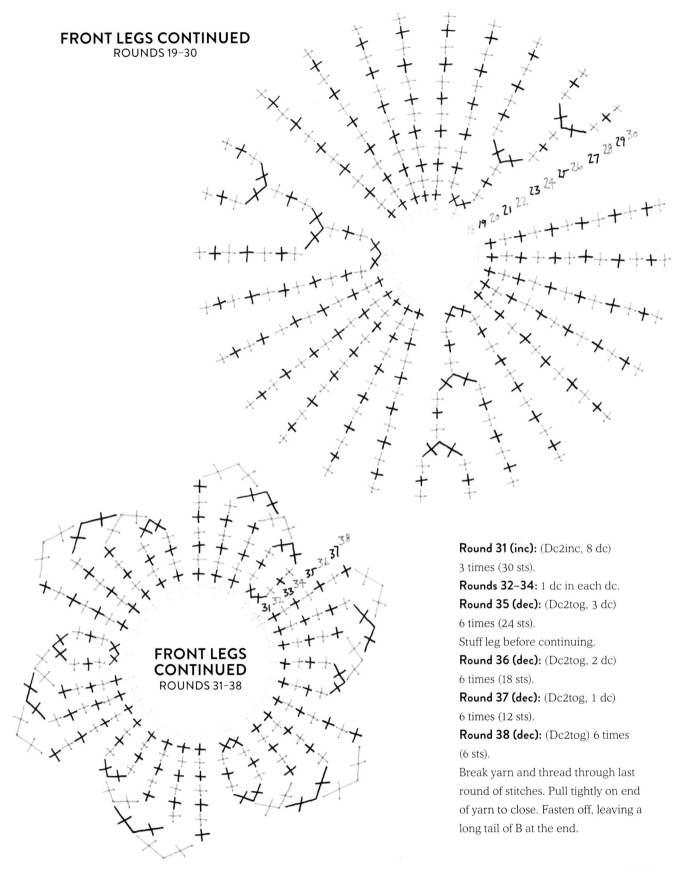

FRONT LEGS CONTINUED
ROUNDS 31–38

Round 31 (inc): (Dc2inc, 8 dc)
3 times (30 sts).

Rounds 32–34: 1 dc in each dc.

Round 35 (dec): (Dc2tog, 3 dc)
6 times (24 sts).

Stuff leg before continuing.

Round 36 (dec): (Dc2tog, 2 dc)
6 times (18 sts).

Round 37 (dec): (Dc2tog, 1 dc)
6 times (12 sts).

Round 38 (dec): (Dc2tog) 6 times
(6 sts).

Break yarn and thread through last
round of stitches. Pull tightly on end
of yarn to close. Fasten off, leaving a
long tail of B at the end.

Hind legs

RIGHT PAW

Starting at the base of the paw, with 3.25mm hook and A, make a magic loop.

Rounds 1–16: Work as for rounds 1–16 of front legs.

SHAPE BACK OF LEG

Round 17: 1 dc in next 3 dc, ending at the side of the leg; 9 ch, skip the 9 dc at the front of the leg, 1 dc in next 6 dc.

Round 18: 1 dc in next 3 dc, 1 dc in next 9 ch, 1 dc in next 6 dc.

Round 19 (dec): (Dc2tog, 1 dc) 6 times (12 sts).

Break yarn and thread through last round of stitches. Pull tightly on end of yarn to close and fasten off.

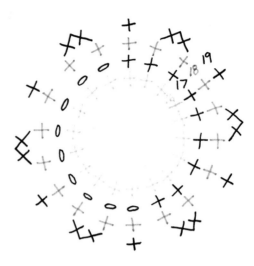

HIND LEGS
SHAPE BACK OF LEG
ROUNDS 17–19

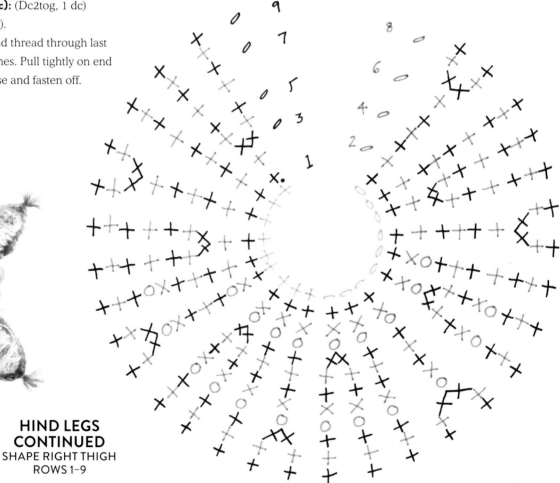

**HIND LEGS
CONTINUED**
SHAPE RIGHT THIGH
ROWS 1–9

58

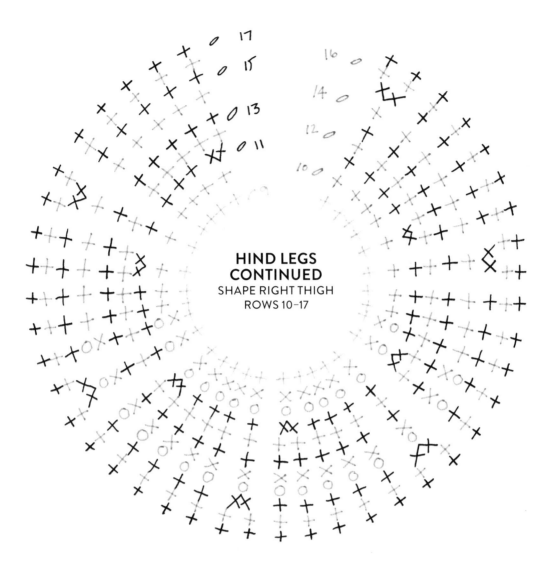

**HIND LEGS
CONTINUED**
SHAPE RIGHT THIGH
ROWS 10–17

SHAPE RIGHT THIGH

With RS of leg facing, 3.25mm hook, join B with a sl st to first of 9 skipped dc of round 16.

Row 1 (RS): 1 dc in same st as sl st, 1 dc in next 8 dc, 1 dc in reverse side of next 9 ch, turn (18 sts).

Row 2 (WS): 1 ch, 1 dc in next 4 dc, 1 lp st in next 9 dc, 1 dc in next 5 dc, turn.

Row 3 (inc): 1 ch, (dc2inc, 2 dc) 6 times, turn (24 sts).

Rows 4–5: 1 ch, 1 dc in each dc, turn.

Row 6: 1 ch, 1 dc in next 6 dc, 1 lp st in next 12 dc, 1 dc in next 6 dc, turn.

Row 7 (inc): 1 ch, (3 dc, dc2inc) 6 times, turn (30 sts).

Rows 8–9: 1 ch, 1 dc in each dc, turn.

Row 10: 1 ch, 1 dc in next 8 dc, 1 lp st in next 14 dc, 1 dc in next 8 dc, turn.

Row 11 (inc): 1 ch, (dc2inc, 4 dc) 6 times, turn (36 sts).

Rows 12–13: 1 ch, 1 dc in each dc, turn.

Row 14: 1 ch, 1 dc in next 10 dc, 1 lp st in next 16 dc, 1 dc in next 10 dc, turn.

Row 15 (inc): 1 ch, (5 dc, dc2inc) 6 times, turn (42 sts).

Rows 16–17: 1 ch, 1 dc in each dc, turn.

Row 18: 1 ch, 1 dc in next 12 dc, 1 lp st in next 18 dc, 1 dc in next 12 dc, turn.

Rows 19–21: 1 ch, 1 dc in each dc, turn.

Row 22: Rep row 18.

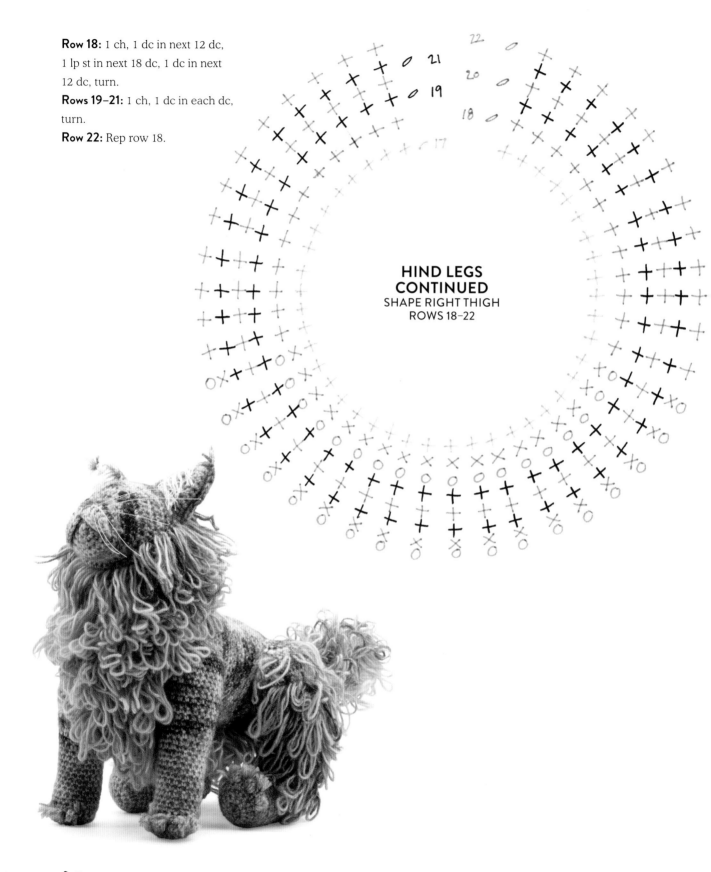

HIND LEGS CONTINUED
SHAPE RIGHT THIGH
ROWS 18–22

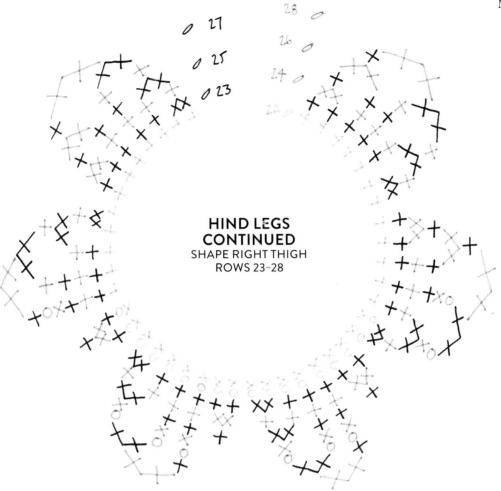

HIND LEGS CONTINUED
SHAPE RIGHT THIGH
ROWS 23–28

Row 23 (dec): 1 ch, (dc2tog, 5 dc) 6 times, turn (36 sts).

Row 24 (dec): 1 ch, (dc2tog, 4 dc) 6 times, turn (30 sts).

Row 25 (dec): 1 ch, (dc2tog, 3 dc) 6 times, turn (24 sts).

Row 26 (dec): 1 ch, dc2tog, 1 dc in next 2 dc, dc2tog, 1 lp st in next 2 dc, (skip next st, 1 lp st in next 3 dc) twice, skip next st, 1 lp st in next dc, 1 dc in next 2 dc, dc2tog, 1 dc in next 2 dc, turn (18 sts).

Row 27 (dec): 1 ch, (dc2tog, 1 dc) 6 times, turn (12 sts).

Row 28 (dec): 1 ch, (dc2tog) 6 times, turn (6 sts).

Fasten off, leaving a long tail of yarn.

LEFT PAW

Starting at the base of the paw, with 3.25mm hook and A, make a magic loop.

Rounds 1–16: Work as for rounds 1–16 of front legs.

SHAPE BACK OF LEG

Rounds 17–19: Work as for rounds 17–19 of right hind leg.

SHAPE LEFT THIGH

With RS of leg facing, 3.25mm hook, join B with a sl st to reverse side of first of 9 ch of round 17.

Row 1 (RS): 1 dc in same st as sl st, 1 dc in reverse side of next 8 ch, 1 dc in next 9 skipped dc of round 16, turn (18 sts).

Rows 2–28: Work as for rows 2–28 of right thigh.

Fasten off, leaving a long tail of yarn at the end.

HIND LEGS CONTINUED
SHAPE LEFT THIGH
ROW 1

Ruff

With 3.25mm hook and A, make 56 ch.

Row 1 (RS): 1 dc in 2nd ch from hook, 1 dc in each ch to end, turn (55 sts).

Row 2 (WS): 1 ch, 1 lp st in each ch to end, turn.

Rows 3–5: 1 ch, 1 dc in each st, turn.

Rows 6–9: Rep rows 2–5.

Row 10: 1 ch, 1 lp st in next 15 dc. Join B in last st and carry unused yarn on WS of work. 1 lp st in next 40 dc with B, turn.

Row 11: 1 ch, 1 dc in next 40 sts with B, 1 dc in next 15 sts with A, turn.

Row 12: 1 ch, 1 dc in next 15 dc with A, 1 dc in next 40 dc with B, turn.

Row 13: Rep row 11.

Row 14: 1 ch, 1 lp st in next 15 dc with A, 1 lp st in next 40 dc with B, turn.

Rows 15–16: Rep rows 11–12.

Row 17 (dec): 1 ch, 1 dc in next 40 sts with B, (dc2tog, 1 dc) 5 times with A, turn (50 sts).

Row 18: 1 ch, 1 lp st in next 10 dc with A, 1 lp st in next 40 dc with B. Fasten off, leaving a long tail each of A and B.

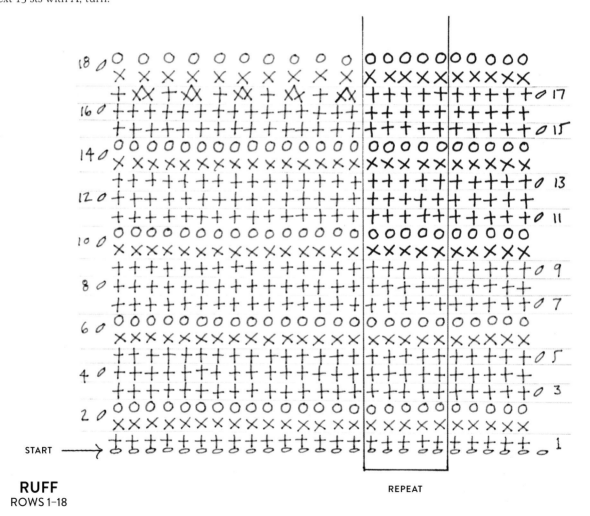

RUFF
ROWS 1–18

REPEAT

START

Tail

With 3.25mm hook and A, make 36 ch.

Row 1 (RS): 1 dc in 2nd ch from hook, 1 dc in next 33 ch, 3 dc in end ch, 1 dc in reverse side of next 34 ch, turn (71 sts).

Row 2 (WS) (inc): 1 ch, 1 lp st in next 35 dc, 3 lp sts in next dc, 1 lp st in next 35 dc, turn (73 sts).

Row 3 (inc): 1 ch, 1 dc in next 36 sts, dc3inc, 1 dc in next 36 sts, turn (75 sts).

Row 4 (inc): 1 ch, 1 dc in next 37 sts, dc3inc, 1 dc in next 37 sts, turn (77 sts).

Row 5 (inc): 1 ch, 1 dc in next 38 sts, dc3inc, 1 dc in next 38 sts, turn (79 sts).

Row 6 (inc): 1 ch, 1 lp st in next 39 dc, 3 lp sts in next dc, 1 lp st in next 39 dc, turn (81 sts).

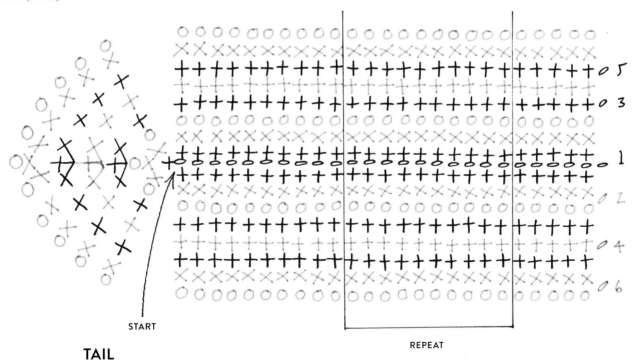

START

TAIL
ROWS 1–6

REPEAT

Row 7 (dec): 1 ch, 1 dc in next 38 sts, dc2tog, 1 dc in next st, dc2tog, 1 dc in next 38 sts. Join B in last dc, turn (79 sts).
Continue with B.

Row 8 (dec): 1 ch, 1 lp st in next 38 dc, skip next dc, 1 lp st in next dc, skip next dc, 1 lp st in next 38 dc, turn (77 sts).

Row 9 (dec): 1 ch, 1 dc in next 12 sts, (dc2tog, 1 dc) 6 times, 1 dc in next 6 sts, dc2tog, 1 dc in next st, dc2tog, 1 dc in next 6 sts, (1 dc, dc2tog) 6 times, 1 dc in next 12 sts, turn (63 sts).

Row 10 (dec): 1 ch, 1 dc in next 29 sts, dc2tog, 1 dc in next st, dc2tog, 1 dc in next 29 sts, turn (61 sts).

Row 11 (dec): 1 ch, 1 dc in next 28 sts, dc2tog, 1 dc in next st, dc2tog, 1 dc in next 28 sts, turn (59 sts).

Row 12 (dec): 1 ch, 1 lp st in next 28 dc, skip next dc, 1 lp st in next dc, skip next dc, 1 lp st in next 28 dc, turn (57 sts).

Fasten off, leaving a long tail of B at the end.

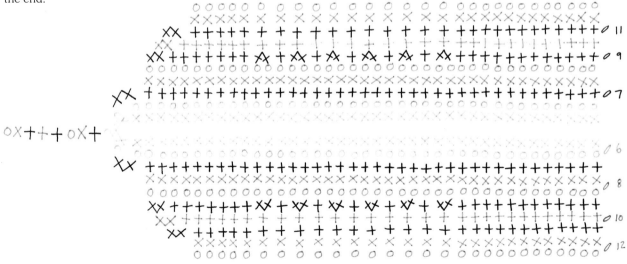

TAIL CONTINUED
ROWS 7–12

Making up

HEAD

Stuff the head. With the tail of yarn left after fastening off, sew the head in place. Stitch all around the neck edges. Tuck the loops that will be covered by the head inside the neck, taking care not to catch the loops that appear around the outside edges of the neck in the stitches. Insert more stuffing into the neck if necessary. Using three strands of embroidery thread, embroider the pupils of the eyes in satin stitch and work straight stitches around each eye to form the irises (see page 170). With B, embroider a fly stitch (see page 170) for the nose and fill it in with satin stitch.

EARS

Stuff the ears lightly, keeping them flat. Sew the ears in place, near the back of the head, stitching all around the lower edges with the tails of yarn left after fastening off. The fur in the ears is made with tassels (see page 171) that are threaded through the posts of the stitches. Use two 4in (10cm) strands of embroidery thread for each tassel. Attach a tassel to seven posts of the stitches of row 2 and eight posts of row 3, nearest the centre of the head, of each inner ear. Trim the ends. For the tuft at the tip of the ears, use three 4in (10cm) lengths of B for each tassel. Attach a tassel to the second of the three stitches at the tip of each ear. Trim the ends.

LEGS

Thread tail of yarn through last row of stitches of the hind legs. Pull tightly on end of yarn to close. Sew the edges of the leg together, matching the rows, stuffing the leg as you sew. Flatten the tops of the hind legs, positioning the seam down the centre of the inside leg, which will be placed against the body. Flatten the tops of the front legs. Sew all the legs in place, stitching all around the top of the thighs with the tails of yarn left after fastening off. Take care not to catch the loops of the hind legs in the stitches. The tufts of fluff on the paws are made in the same way as for the ears. Use two 4in (10cm) lengths of A for each tassel. Attach a tassel to the two stitches between each toe on the front and back feet. Trim the ends.

TAIL

Using the length of yarn left after fastening off, fold the tail lengthways and sew the long edges together with whip stitch (see page 169). Stuff the tail lightly, keeping a flattened shape. Sew the tail in place, stitching all around the edges.

RUFF

Sew the short edges of the ruff together, matching the rows. Slip the ruff over the head. Align the section of the ruff worked in A with the front of the head, under the chin, and position the back of the ruff to match the line of stitches behind the ears. Use the tails of yarn left after fastening off to sew the last row of the ruff to the head, stitching it in place all around the edges. Attach tassels to each side of the face, next to the last row of the ruff, starting in front of the edge of each ear and finishing at the section of the ruff worked in A. Use one 4in (10cm) length of B for each tassel. Trim the ends of the tassels to neaten, taking care not to cut into the loops of the ruff.

WHISKERS (OPTIONAL)

Attach three whiskers to the posts of the stitches on each side of the muzzle (see page 171). Trim the ends. Weave in all the yarn ends.

Siamese

THE COMBINATION OF GREYS, IN SOLID AND MIXED SHADES, ARE USED
TO CREATE THE GRADUATED COLOURING ON THE FACE AND LEGS OF
THIS SITTING SIAMESE BLUE POINT.

Materials

- Drops Karisma, 100% wool (109yd/100m per 50g
  ball), or any DK yarn:
  1 x 50g ball in 16 Dark Grey Mix (A)
  1 x 50g ball in 21 Medium Grey Mix (B)
  1 x 50g ball in 44 Light Grey Mix (C)
  1 x 50g ball in 72 Light Pearl Grey (D)
- Stranded embroidery thread in blue, such as DMC
  Stranded Cotton, shade 813, for the eyes
- Metallic stranded embroidery thread in black,
  such as DMC Light Effects, shade E310, for the
  nose and the pupils of the eyes
- 6 lengths of 0.3mm clear nylon thread, each
  measuring 4¾in (12cm), for the optional whiskers
  (not suitable for young children)
- 3.25mm (UK10:USD/3) crochet hook
- Blunt-ended yarn needle
- Toy stuffing
- Stitch marker

Size

- Approximately 4⅜in (13.5cm) long, from tip of
  nose to back of hind legs
- Approximately 6⅞in (17.5cm) tall from top of head
  (excluding ears)

Tension

22 sts and 24 rows to 4in (10cm) over double crochet
using 3.25mm hook. Use a larger or smaller hook if
necessary to obtain the correct tension.

Method

The sitting Siamese cat's head, neck and body are worked in one piece, in rounds and rows of double crochet. The shading on the face and legs is formed by changing the yarn to a lighter shade for subsequent rounds. The front of the head is crocheted in rounds and the top of the head is worked in rows. The neck is worked in rows, crocheting along the edges of the rows that make up the top of the head and into the stitches at the underside of the muzzle. The shaping of the body is crocheted in short rows, working into just a few stitches of the previous row and then crocheting into an unworked stitch at the end of each subsequent row. The ears are worked in rows. Each ear is made up of two identical crocheted parts that are joined by crocheting into each stitch of both pieces at the same time. Double crochet and half treble stitches form the tapered shape of the tail, decreasing the stitches in the last row to form the curl. The long edges of the tail are sewn together, and a small amount of stuffing is inserted before sewing it in place. The toes on the paws are produced by crocheting bobbles. The bobbles appear on the reverse side of the fabric. The thighs of the hind legs should be lightly stuffed so they have some flexibility and can easily bend into the sitting position. The eyes and nose are embroidered with stranded embroidery threads.

1 ch and 2 ch at beg of the row/round does not count as a st throughout.

Head and Body

HEAD
Starting at front of muzzle, with 3.25mm hook and A, make a magic loop (see page 163).

Round 1: 1 ch, 6 dc into loop (6 sts).

Round 2 (inc): (Dc2inc) 6 times (12 sts). Pull tightly on short end of yarn to close loop.

Rounds 3–4: 1 dc in each dc.

Round 5: (Dc2inc, 1 dc) 6 times. Join B in last dc (18 sts).

Round 6: With B, 1 dc in each dc.

Round 7 (inc): (1 dc, dc2inc) 6 times, 1 dc in next 6 dc. Join C in last dc (24 sts).

Round 8 (inc): (1 dc, dc2inc, 1 dc) 6 times finishing 6 sts before the end, turn (30 sts).

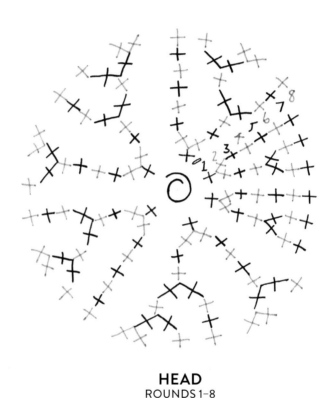

HEAD
ROUNDS 1–8

KEY

⟋ CHAIN (CH)

● SLIP STITCH (SL ST)

+ DOUBLE CROCHET (DC)

⤬ DC2INC

⤬ DC2TOG

⤛ DC6TOG

⊕ MAKE BOBBLE (MB)

TOP OF HEAD

Row 1 (WS): 1 ch, 1 dc in next 24 dc. Join D in last dc, turn. Continue with D on these 24 sts.

Row 2 (RS): 1 ch, 1 dc in each dc, turn.

Rows 3–5: Rep last row.

Row 6 (dec): 1 ch, (dc2tog, 2 dc) 6 times, turn (18 sts).

Row 7 (dec): 1 ch, (dc2tog, 1 dc) 6 times, turn (12 sts).

Row 8 (dec): 1 ch, (dc2tog) 6 times (6 sts).

Row 9: 1 ch, dc6tog (insert the hook into the next st, yrh and draw back through the stitch 6 times (7 loops on hook), yrh and draw through all 7 loops on the hook, turn (1 st).

TOP OF HEAD
ROW 9

NECK

Row 1 (RS): 1 ch, rotate head and work 7 dc evenly along edge of the rows of head, 1 dc in next 6 unworked dc of round 7 of head, work 7 dc evenly along edge of rows of head, sl st to first dc, turn (20 sts).

Row 2 (WS): 1 dc in each dc, turn.

Row 3 (inc): 1 ch, (2 dc, dc2inc, 2 dc) 4 times, sl st to first dc, turn (24 sts).

Row 4: 1 dc in each dc, turn.

Row 5: 1 ch, 1 dc in each dc, sl st to first dc, turn.

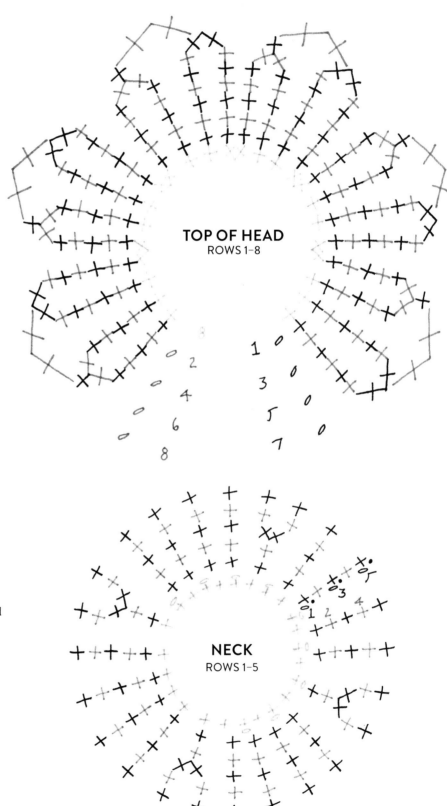

TOP OF HEAD
ROWS 1–8

NECK
ROWS 1–5

SHAPE FRONT OF BODY

Row 1 (WS): 1 dc in next 14 dc, sl st in next dc, turn.

Row 2 (RS) (inc): 1 dc in same st as sl st, 1 dc in next dc, (dc2inc) twice, 1 dc in next 2 dc, sl st in next dc, turn (26 sts).

Row 3: 1 dc in same st as sl st, 1 dc in next 9 dc, sl st in next dc, turn.

Row 4 (inc): 1 dc in same st as sl st, 1 dc in next 4 dc, (dc2inc) twice, 1 dc in next 5 dc, sl st in next dc, turn (28 sts).

Row 5: 1 dc in same st as sl st, 1 dc in next 15 dc, sl st in next dc, turn.

Row 6 (inc): 1 dc in same st as sl st, 1 dc in next 7 dc, (dc2inc) twice, 1 dc in next 8 dc, sl st in next dc, turn (30 sts).

Row 7: 1 dc in same st as sl st, 1 dc in next 21 dc, sl st in next dc, turn.

Row 8: 1 dc in same st as sl st, 1 dc in next 23 dc, sl st in next dc, turn.

Row 9: 1 dc in same st as sl st, 1 dc in next 25 dc, sl st in next dc, turn.

Row 10: 1 dc in same st as sl st, 1 dc in next 27 dc, sl st in next dc, turn.

Row 11: 1 dc in same st as sl st, 1 dc in next 29 dc, sl st to first dc, turn. Stuff head and neck before continuing.

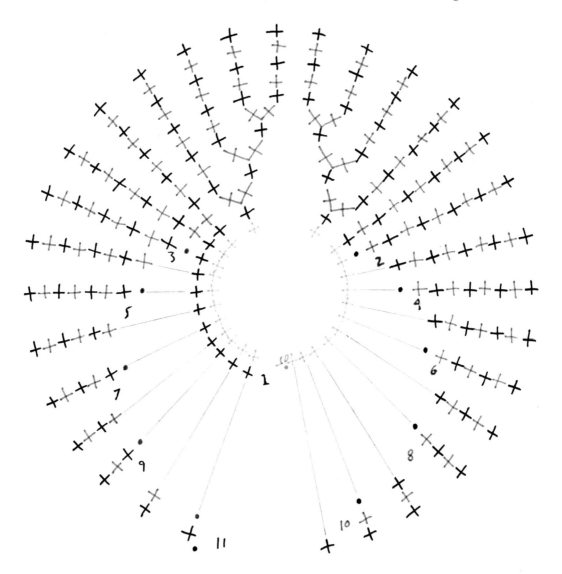

SHAPE FRONT OF BODY
ROWS 1–11

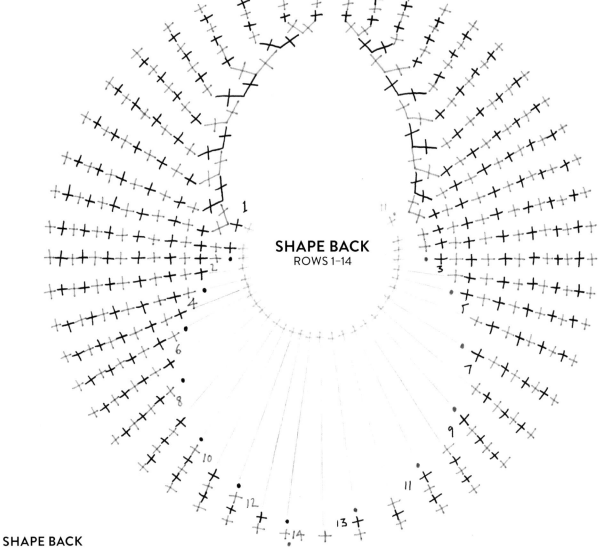

SHAPE BACK
ROWS 1–14

SHAPE BACK

Row 1 (RS): 1 dc in next 2 dc, sl st in next dc, turn.

Row 2 (WS) (inc): 1 dc in same st as sl st, 1 dc in next dc, (dc2inc) twice, 1 dc in next 2 dc, sl st in next dc, turn (32 sts).

Row 3 (inc): 1 dc in same st as sl st, 1 dc in next 3 dc, (dc2inc) twice, 1 dc in next 4 dc, sl st in next dc, turn (34 sts).

Row 4 (inc): 1 dc in same st as sl st, 1 dc in next 5 dc, (dc2inc) twice, 1 dc in next 6 dc, sl st in next dc, turn (36 sts).

Row 5 (inc): 1 dc in same st as sl st, 1 dc in next 7 dc, (dc2inc) twice, 1 dc in next 8 dc, sl st in next dc, turn (38 sts).

Row 6 (inc): 1 dc in same st as sl st, 1 dc in next 9 dc, (dc2inc) twice, 1 dc in next 10 dc, sl st in next dc, turn (40 sts).

Row 7 (inc): 1 dc in same st as sl st, 1 dc in next 11 dc, (dc2inc) twice, 1 dc in next 12 dc, sl st in next dc, turn (42 sts).

Row 8 (inc): 1 dc in same st as sl st, 1 dc in next 13 dc, (dc2inc) twice, 1 dc in next 14 dc, sl st in next dc, turn (44 sts).

Row 9 (inc): 1 dc in same st as sl st, 1 dc in next 15 dc, (dc2inc) twice,

1 dc in next 16 dc, sl st in next dc, turn (46 sts).

Row 10 (inc): 1 dc in same st as sl st, 1 dc in next 17 dc, (dc2inc) twice, 1 dc in next 18 dc, sl st in next dc, turn (48 sts).

Row 11: 1 dc in same st as sl st, 1 dc in next 41 dc, sl st in next dc, turn.

Row 12: 1 dc in same st as sl st, 1 dc in next 43 dc, sl st in next dc, turn.

Row 13: 1 dc in same st as sl st, 1 dc in next 45 dc, sl st in next dc, turn.

Row 14: 1 dc in same st as sl st, 1 dc in next 47 dc, sl st to first dc, turn.

SHAPE MIDDLE OF BODY

Row 1 (RS) (dec): 1 dc in next 4 dc, dc2tog, 1 dc in next 36 dc, dc2tog, 1 dc in next 4 dc, turn (46 sts).

Row 2 (WS) (dec): 1 ch, 1 dc in next 4 dc, dc2tog, 1 dc in next 34 dc, dc2tog, 1 dc in next 4 dc, sl st to first dc, turn (44 sts).

Row 3 (dec): 1 dc in next 4 dc, dc2tog, 1 dc in next 32 dc, dc2tog, 1 dc in next 4 dc, turn (42 sts).

Row 4 (dec): 1 ch, 1 dc in next 4 dc, dc2tog, 1 dc in next 30 dc, dc2tog, 1 dc in next 4 dc, sl st to first dc, turn (40 sts).

Row 5 (dec): 1 dc in next 4 dc, dc2tog, 1 dc in next 28 dc, dc2tog, 1 dc in next 4 dc, turn (38 sts).

Row 6 (dec): 1 ch, 1 dc in next 4 dc, dc2tog, 1 dc in next 26 dc, dc2tog, 1 dc in next 4 dc, sl st to first dc, turn (36 sts).

Row 7 (dec): 1 dc in next 4 dc, dc2tog, 1 dc in next 24 dc, dc2tog, 1 dc in next 4 dc, turn (34 sts).

Row 8 (dec): 1 ch, 1 dc in next 4 dc, dc2tog, 1 dc in next 22 dc, dc2tog, 1 dc in next 4 dc, sl st to first dc, turn (32 sts).

Row 9 (dec): 1 dc in next 4 dc, dc2tog, 1 dc in next 20 dc, dc2tog, 1 dc in next 4 dc, turn (30 sts).

Row 10: 1 ch, 1 dc in each dc, sl st to first dc, turn.

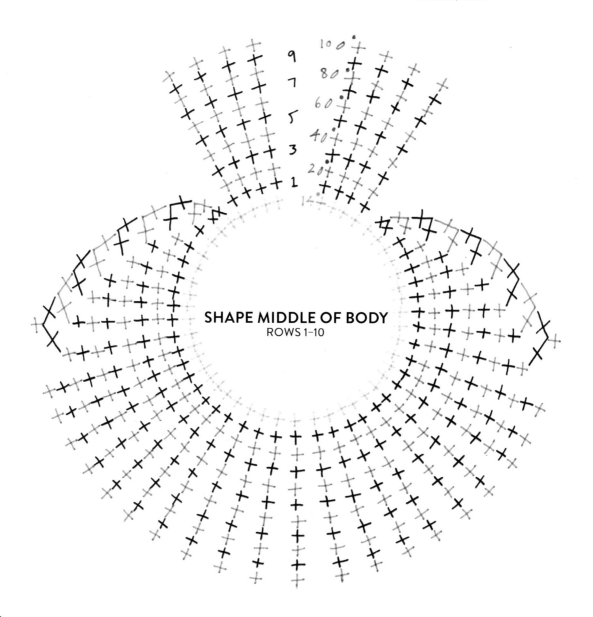

SHAPE MIDDLE OF BODY
ROWS 1–10

SHAPE END OF BODY

The following is worked in rounds.

Round 1 (dec): (Dc2tog, 3 dc) 6 times (24 sts).

Stuff body before continuing.

Round 2 (dec): (Dc2tog, 2 dc) 6 times (18 sts).

Round 3 (dec): (Dc2tog, 1 dc) 6 times (12 sts).

Round 4 (dec): (Dc2tog) 6 times (6 sts).

Break yarn and thread through last 6 stitches. Pull tightly on end of yarn to close. Fasten off.

Ears (make 2)

With 3.25mm hook and B, make 5 ch.

Row 1: 1 dc in 2nd ch from hook, 1 dc in next 2 ch, 3 dc in next ch, 1 dc in reverse side of next 3 ch, turn (9 sts).

Row 2 (inc): 1 ch, dc2inc, 1 dc in next 3 dc, dc3inc, 1 dc in next 3 dc, dc2inc. (13 sts).

Fasten off, leaving a long tail of yarn. This completes the inner ear.

With A, make one more piece to match the first for the outer ear. Turn work at the end and do not fasten off.

JOIN EAR PIECES

Place the two ear pieces together, with the inner ear facing up.

Next: 1 ch, inserting the hook under both loops of each stitch of the inner ear first, then the outer ear at the same time to join, dc2inc, 1 dc in next 5 dc, dc3inc, 1 dc in next 5 dc, dc2inc (17 sts). Fasten off, leaving a long tail of yarn.

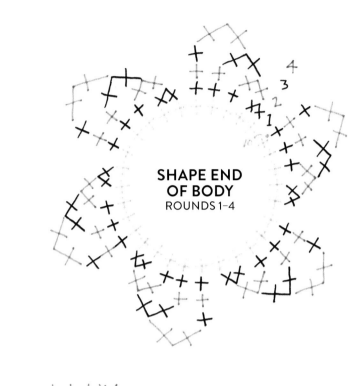

SHAPE END OF BODY
ROUNDS 1–4

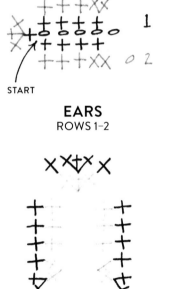

START

EARS
ROWS 1–2

NEXT

JOIN EAR PIECES
INSERT HOOK INTO EACH STITCH OF BOTH EAR PIECES AT SAME TIME TO JOIN

Front legs (make 2)

The bobbles appear on the reverse side of the work. This will be the right side. See page 166 for instructions to make bobble (mb).

Starting at the base of the paw, with 3.25mm hook and A, make a magic loop.

Round 1 (WS): 1 ch, 6 dc into loop (6 sts).

Round 2 (inc): (Dc2inc) 6 times (12 sts). Pull tightly on short end of yarn to close loop.

Round 3 (inc): 1 dc in next 7 dc, (dc2inc, 1 dc) twice, 1 dc in next dc (14 sts).

Round 4: 1 dc in next 6 dc, (mb, 1 dc in next dc) 4 times, turn.

FRONT LEGS
ROUNDS 1–4

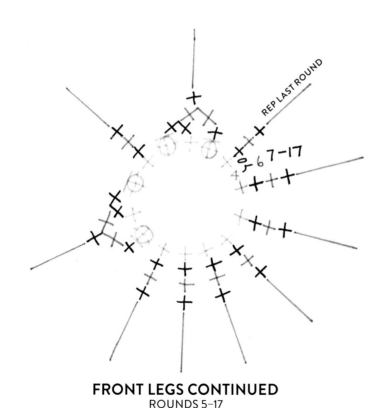

FRONT LEGS CONTINUED
ROUNDS 5–17

Round 5 (RS) (dec): 1 ch, 1 dc in first dc, (1 dc in next st, dc2tog) twice, 1 dc in next 7 dc (12 sts).

Round 6 (dec): (1 dc in next dc, dc2tog) twice, 1 dc in next 6 dc (10 sts).

Round 7: 1 dc in each dc. Join B in last dc.

Rounds 8–15: 1 dc in each dc with B. Join C in last dc of round 15.

Rounds 16–17: 1 dc in each dc with C. Join D in last dc of round 17. Continue with D.

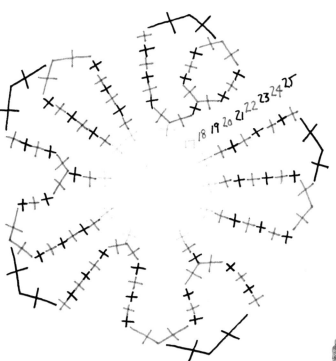

FRONT LEGS CONTINUED
ROUNDS 18–25

Round 18 (inc): (Dc2inc, 4 dc) twice (12 sts).

Round 19: 1 dc in each dc.

Round 20 (inc): (Dc2inc, 3 dc) 3 times (15 sts).

Rounds 21–23: 1 dc in each dc. Stuff leg before continuing.

Round 24 (dec): (Dc2tog, 1 dc) 5 times (10 sts).

Round 25 (dec): (Dc2tog) 5 times (5 sts).

Break yarn and thread through last round of stitches. Pull tightly on end of yarn to close and fasten off, leaving a long tail of D.

Hind legs (make 2)

Follow charts for the sleeping Russian Blue's hind legs on pages 143–4. Starting at the front of the paw, with 3.25mm hook and A, make 6 ch.

Round 1 (WS): 1 dc in 2nd ch from hook, (mb, 1 dc in next ch) twice, 1 dc in reverse side of each ch to end (10 sts).

Round 2 (inc): 1 dc in next dc, mb in same st as last dc, 1 dc in next 3 dc, mb, 1 dc in same st as last st, dc2inc, 1 dc in next 3 dc, dc2inc, turn (14 sts).

Round 3 (RS): 1 ch, 1 dc in each st.

Round 4: 1 dc in each dc. Join B in last dc.

Continue with B.

Rounds 5–6: 1 dc in each dc.

Round 7 (dec): (1 dc, dc2tog) twice, 1 dc in next 8 dc (12 sts).

Round 8: 1 dc in each dc.

Round 9 (dec): (Dc2tog, 1 dc) twice, 1 dc in next 6 dc (10 sts).

Rounds 10–14: 1 dc in each dc.

SHAPE BACK OF LEG

Round 15: 1 dc in next 2 dc, ending at the side of the leg; 5 ch, skip the 5 dc at the front of the leg, 1 dc in next 3 dc.

Round 16: 1 dc in next 2 dc, 1 dc in next 5 ch, 1 dc in next 3 dc. Break yarn and thread through last round of stitches. Pull tightly on end of yarn to close and fasten off.

SHAPE THIGH

With RS of leg facing, 3.25mm hook, join B with a sl st to first of 5 skipped dc.

Round 1: 1 dc in same st as sl st, 1 dc in next 4 dc, 1 dc in reverse side of next 5 ch (10 sts).

Round 2 (inc): (Dc2inc, 1 dc) 5 times (15 sts).

Round 3 (inc): (Dc2inc, 2 dc) 5 times. Join C in last dc (20 sts).

Round 4 (inc): With C, (dc2inc, 3 dc) 5 times (25 sts).

Round 5 (inc): (Dc2inc, 4 dc) 5 times. Join D in last dc (30 sts).

Continue with D.

Rounds 6–11: 1 dc in each dc.

Round 12 (dec): (Dc2tog, 3 dc) 6 times (24 sts).

Stuff the leg and lightly stuff the thigh before continuing.

Round 13 (dec): (Dc2tog, 2 dc) 6 times (18 sts).

Round 14 (dec): (Dc2tog, 1 dc) 6 times (12 sts).

Round 15 (dec): (Dc2tog) 6 times (6 sts).

Break yarn and thread through last round of stitches. Pull tightly on end of yarn to close and fasten off, leaving a long tail of D.

Tail

With 3.25mm hook and A, make 31 ch.

Row 1: 1 dc in 2nd ch from hook, 1 dc in next 28 ch, 3 dc in end ch, 1 dc in reverse side of next 29 ch, turn (61 sts).

Row 2 (dec): 2 ch, 1 htr in next 8 dc, 1 dc in next 2 dc, (dc2tog, 1 dc) 4 times, 1 dc in next 8 dc, dc3inc, 1 dc in next 8 dc, (1 dc, dc2tog) 4 times, 1 dc in next 2 dc, 1 htr in next 8 dc (55 sts). Fasten off, leaving a long tail of yarn at the end.

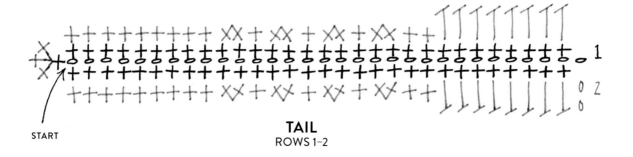

START

TAIL
ROWS 1–2

Making up

HEAD

Embroider the nose in satin stitch (see page 170) using three strands of metallic embroidery thread. With the thread used for the nose, embroider the pupils of the eyes. Work straight stitches around the pupils to form the irises (see page 170).

EARS

Stuff the ears lightly, keeping them flat. Sew the ears in place, near the back of the head, stitching all around the lower edges with the tails of yarn left after fastening off.

LEGS

Flatten the top of the legs and sew in place, stitching all around the top of the thighs with the tail of yarn left after fastening off.

TAIL

Using the length of yarn left after fastening off, fold the tail lengthways and sew the long edges together with whip stitch (see page 169). Use the end of the crochet hook to push a small amount of stuffing into the tail. Sew the tail in place, so it curls up or wraps around the side of the body.

WHISKERS (OPTIONAL)

Attach three whiskers to the posts of the stitches on each side of the muzzle (see page 171). Trim the ends. Weave in all the yarn ends.

Exotic Shorthair

THE DISTINCTIVE FACIAL FEATURES OF THIS EXOTIC SHORTHAIR ARE FORMED BY WORKING VARIOUS STITCHES OF DIFFERENT LENGTHS FOR THE MUZZLE AND POSITIONING THE EMBROIDERED DETAILS CLOSE TOGETHER.

Materials

- Sirdar Haworth Tweed, 50% merino wool, 50% nylon (180yd/165m per 50g ball), or any DK yarn:
  1 x 50g ball in F001-0911 Cotton Grass Cream (A)
  1 x 50g ball in F001-0910 Harewood Chestnut (B)
- Stranded embroidery thread in brown, such as Anchor Stranded Cotton, shade 0944, for the eyes
- Stranded embroidery thread in black, such as Anchor Stranded Cotton, shade 0403, for the pupils
- Stranded embroidery thread in pink, such as Anchor Stranded Cotton, shade 0969, for the nose
- 6 lengths of 0.3mm clear nylon thread, each measuring 4¾in (12cm), for the optional whiskers (not suitable for young children)
- 3.25mm (UK10:USD/3) crochet hook
- Blunt-ended yarn needle
- Toy stuffing

Size

- Approximately 6½in (16.5cm) body length, from tip of nose to back of hind legs
- Approximately 6⅛in (15.5cm) tall from top of head (excluding ears)

Tension

21 sts and 22 rows to 4in (10cm) over double crochet using 3.25mm hook. Use a larger or smaller hook if necessary to obtain the correct tension.

Method

The cat's head, body and legs are worked in rounds and rows of double crochet, using two colours. The first row of the muzzle is crocheted into the front loops of the previous row, and the shaping is formed by a combination of double crochet, half treble, treble and slip stitches. The unworked back loops are crocheted to begin the rest of the head shaping. The neck is worked in rows, with two colours, starting by crocheting into the stitches at the underside of the muzzle, and then along the edges of the rows that make up the top of the head. The ears are worked in rows. Each ear is made up of two crocheted parts that are joined by crocheting into each stitch of both pieces at the same time. The curve in the tail is formed by working double crochet and half treble stitches at the back of the tail on alternate rows. The legs are worked in continuous rounds of double crochet. The toes on the paws are produced by crocheting bobbles. The bobbles appear on the reverse side of the fabric, so the work is turned after crocheting the toes and continued on the right side. The eyes and nose are embroidered using stranded embroidery threads.

1 ch and 2 ch at beg of the row/round does not count as a st throughout.

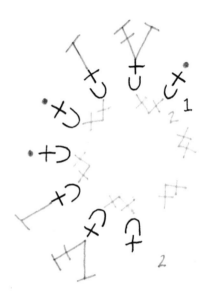

MUZZLE
ROUNDS 1–2

Muzzle

With 3.25mm hook and A, make a magic loop (see page 163).
Round 1: 1 ch, 6 dc into loop (6 sts).
Round 2 (inc): (Dc2inc) 6 times (12 sts). Pull tightly on short end of yarn to close loop.

SHAPE FRONT OF MUZZLE
Row 1: 1 dc in front loop only of next 8 sts, turn.
Row 2: Skip first dc, (1 htr, 1 tr) in next dc, 1 htr in next dc, sl st in next 2 dc, 1 htr in next dc, (1 tr, 1 htr) in next dc. Join B in last dc and carry unused yarn on WS of work, sl st to next dc with B, turn.

SHAPE FRONT OF MUZZLE
ROUNDS 1–2

COLOUR KEY FOR YARNS

FOR SHAPE FACE, NECK, SHAPE MIDDLE OF BODY, TAIL STRIPES
All other charts are shown in alternate rounds/rows of blue and black.

KEY

⟲ MAGIC LOOP

∂ CHAIN (CH)

• SLIP STITCH (SL ST)

+ DOUBLE CROCHET (DC)

⤬ DC2INC

⤨ DC3INC

⤬ DC2TOG

⊤ HALF TREBLE (HTR)

⊥ TREBLE (HTR)

⊕ MAKE BOBBLE (MB)

∩ WORK INTO BACK LOOP ONLY

∪ WORK INTO FRONT LOOP ONLY

SHAPE FACE

Row 1 (RS): Working in the unworked back loops of round 2 of muzzle, 1 dc in next 8 dc with B, 1 dc in both loops of next 4 dc with A, turn.

Row 2 (WS) (inc): 1 ch, 1 dc in next dc, (dc2inc) twice, 1 dc in next dc with A; with B, (dc2inc, 1 dc) twice, (1 dc, dc2inc) twice, sl st to first dc, turn (18 sts).

Row 3 (inc): (Dc2inc, 1 dc) 6 times with B, 1 dc in next 6 dc with A, turn (24 sts).

Row 4 (inc): 1 ch, 1 dc in next 6 dc with A, (dc2inc, 2 dc) 6 times with B, sl st to first dc, turn (30 sts).

Row 5: 1 dc in next 24 dc with B, finishing 6 sts before the end, turn. Continue with B. Do not fasten off A.

TOP OF HEAD

Row 6 (WS): 1 ch, 1 dc in next 24 dc, turn.

Continue on these 24 sts.

Row 7 (RS): 1 ch, 1 dc in each dc, turn.

Rows 8–10: Rep row 7.

Row 11 (dec): (Dc2tog, 2 dc) 6 times, turn (18 sts).

Row 12 (dec): (Dc2tog, 1 dc) 6 times, turn (12 sts).

Row 13 (dec): (Dc2tog) 6 times, turn (6 sts).

Break yarn and thread through last 6 stitches. Pull tightly on end of yarn. Fasten off.

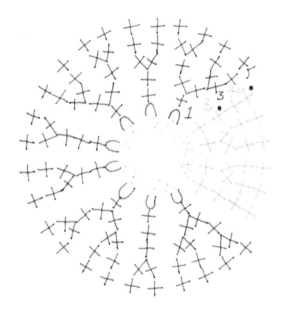

SHAPE FACE
ROWS 1–5

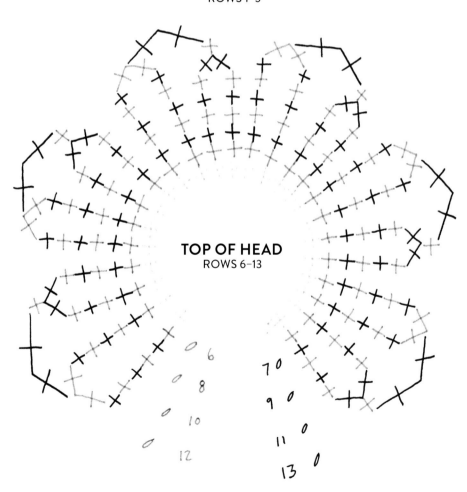

TOP OF HEAD
ROWS 6–13

NECK

With RS of head facing, 3.25mm hook and A, sl st to first of unworked 6 dc of row 4 of shape face.

Row 1 (RS): 1 dc in same st as sl st, 1 dc in next 5 dc. Join B in last dc and carry unused yarn on WS of work. With B, work 14 dc evenly along edge of the rows of head, sl st to first dc, turn (20 sts).

Row 2 (WS) (inc): *(1 dc, dc2inc, 1 dc) twice*, 1 dc in next 2 dc; rep from * to * with B; rep from * to * with A, turn (26 sts).

Row 3: With A, 1 ch, 1 dc in next 8 dc; with B, 1 dc in next 18 dc, sl st to first dc and fasten off, leaving a long tail each of A and B.

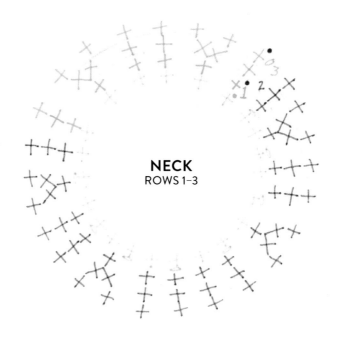

NECK
ROWS 1–3

Ears (make 2)

With 3.25mm hook and A, make 3 ch.
Row 1: 1 dc in 2nd ch from hook, 3 dc in end ch, 1 dc in reverse side of next ch, turn (5 sts).
Fasten off, leaving a long tail of yarn. This completes the inner ear.
With B, make one more piece to match the first for the outer ear. Turn work at the end and do not fasten off.

JOIN EAR PIECES

Place the two ear pieces together, with the inner ear facing up.
Next: 1 ch, inserting the hook under both loops of each stitch of the inner ear first, then the outer ear at the same time to join, (dc2inc, 1 dc) twice, dc2inc (8 sts). Fasten off, leaving a long tail of yarn.

START

EARS
ROW 1

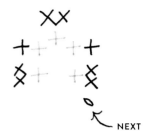

NEXT

JOIN EAR PIECES
INSERT HOOK INTO EACH
STITCH OF BOTH PIECES AT
SAME TIME TO JOIN

Body

SHAPE FRONT

Starting at front of body, with 3.25mm hook and A, make a magic loop.

Round 1: 1 ch, 6 dc into loop (6 sts).

Round 2 (inc): (Dc2inc) 6 times (12 sts). Pull tightly on short end of yarn to close loop.

Round 3 (inc): (Dc2inc, 1 dc) 6 times (18 sts).

Rounds 4–6 (inc): Continue increasing 6 sts on each round as set until there are 36 sts.

Rounds 7–17: 1 dc in each dc.

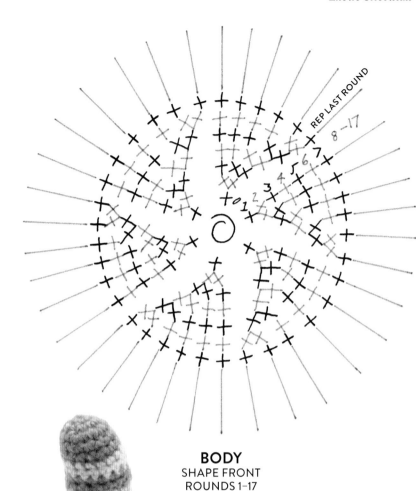

BODY
SHAPE FRONT
ROUNDS 1–17

SHAPE MIDDLE OF BODY

The following is worked in rows.

Row 1 (RS): 1 dc in next 21 dc. Join B in last dc and carry unused yarn on WS of work, 1 dc in next 12 dc with B, 1 dc in next 3 dc with A, turn.

Row 2 (WS): 1 ch, 1 dc in next 2 dc with A, 1 dc in next 14 dc with B, 1 dc in next 20 dc with A, sl st to first dc, turn.

Row 3: 1 dc in next 19 dc with A, 1 dc in next 16 dc with B, 1 dc in next dc with A, turn.

Row 4: With B, 1 ch, 1 dc in next 18 dc; with A, 1 dc in next 18 dc, sl st to first dc, turn.

Row 5: 1 dc in next 18 dc with A, 1 dc in next 18 dc with B, turn.

Rows 6–13: Rep rows 4–5 4 times.

Row 14 (dec): 1 ch, *(dc2tog, 4 dc) 3 times* with B; rep from * to * with A, sl st to first dc, turn (30 sts).

Row 15 (dec): *(Dc2tog, 3 dc) 3 times* with A; rep from * to * with B, do not turn (24 sts).

Stuff body before continuing.

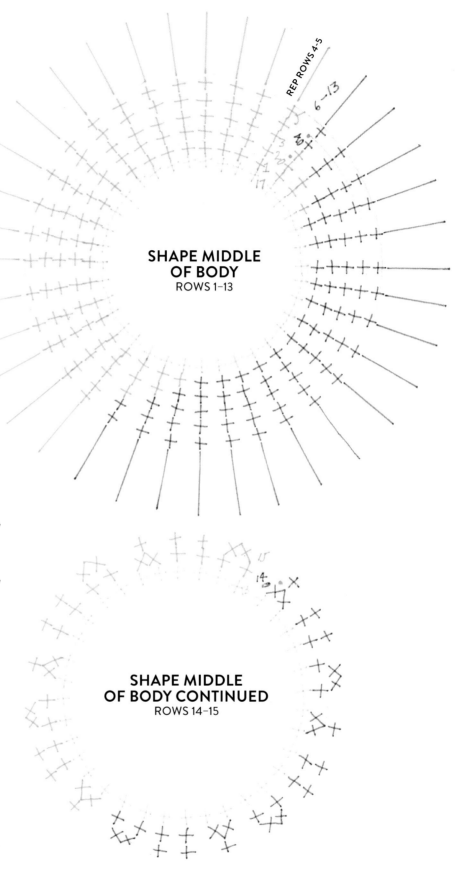

SHAPE MIDDLE OF BODY
ROWS 1–13

SHAPE MIDDLE OF BODY CONTINUED
ROWS 14–15

SHAPE END OF BODY

The following is worked in rounds.
Continue with B.

Round 1 (dec): (Dc2tog, 2 dc) 6 times
(18 sts).

Round 2 (dec): (Dc2tog, 1 dc) 6 times
(12 sts).

Round 3 (dec): (Dc2tog) 6 times
(6 sts).

Break yarn and thread through last
6 stitches.

Pull tightly on end of yarn to close.

Fasten off.

**SHAPE END
OF BODY**
ROUNDS 1–3

FRONT LEGS
ROUNDS 1–4

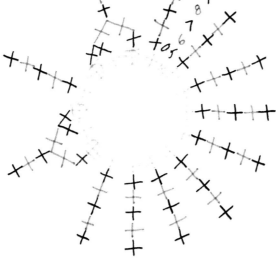

FRONT LEGS CONTINUED
ROUNDS 5–9

Front legs (make 2)

The bobbles appear on the reverse
side of the work. This will be the right
side. See page 166 for instructions to
make bobble (mb).

Starting at the base of the paw, with
3.25mm hook and A, make a magic
loop.

Round 1 (WS): 1 ch, 6 dc into loop
(6 sts).

Round 2 (inc): (Dc2inc) 6 times
(12 sts). Pull tightly on short end of
yarn to close loop.

Round 3 (inc): (Dc2inc, 2 dc) 4 times
(16 sts).

Round 4: 1 dc in next 8 dc, (mb, 1 dc
in next dc) 4 times, turn.

Round 5 (RS) (dec): 1 ch, 1 dc in first
dc, (1 dc in next st, dc2tog) twice,
1 dc in next 9 dc (14 sts).

Round 6 (dec): (1 dc in next dc,
dc2tog) twice, 1 dc in next 8 dc
(12 sts).

Rounds 7–9: 1 dc in each dc.

Round 10 (inc): (Dc2inc, 3 dc) 3 times (15 sts).

Rounds 11–14: 1 dc in each dc.

Round 15 (inc): (Dc2inc, 4 dc) 3 times (18 sts).

Rounds 16–19: 1 dc in each dc.

Stuff leg before continuing.

Round 20 (dec): (Dc2tog, 1 dc) 6 times (12 sts).

Round 21 (dec): (Dc2tog) 6 times (6 sts).

Break yarn and thread through last round of stitches. Pull tightly on end of yarn to close. Fasten off, leaving a long tail of yarn.

FRONT LEGS CONTINUED
ROUNDS 10–15

FRONT LEGS CONTINUED
ROUNDS 16–21

Hind legs

Starting at the base of the paw, with 3.25mm hook and A, make a magic loop.

Rounds 1–9: Work as for rounds 1–9 of front legs.

SHAPE BACK OF LEG

Round 10: 1 dc in each dc.

Round 11: 1 dc in next dc, ending at the side of the leg; 6 ch, skip the 6 dc at the front of the leg, 1 dc in next 5 dc.

Round 12: 1 dc in next dc, 1 dc in next 6 ch, 1 dc in next 5 dc.

Break yarn and thread through last round of stitches. Pull tightly on end of yarn to close and fasten off.

HIND LEGS
SHAPE BACK OF LEG
ROUNDS 10–12

SHAPE THIGH

With RS of leg facing, 3.25mm hook, and A, sl st in first of skipped 6 dc of round 12.

Round 1: 1 dc in same st as sl st, 1 dc in next 5 dc, 1 dc in reverse side of next 6 ch (12 sts).

Round 2: 1 dc in each dc. Join B in last dc.

Continue with B.

Round 3 (inc): (Dc2inc, 1 dc) 6 times (18 sts).

Rounds 4–5: 1 dc in each dc.

Round 6 (inc): (Dc2inc, 2 dc) 6 times (24 sts).

Rounds 7–8: 1 dc in each dc.

Round 9 (inc): (Dc2inc, 3 dc) 6 times (30 sts).

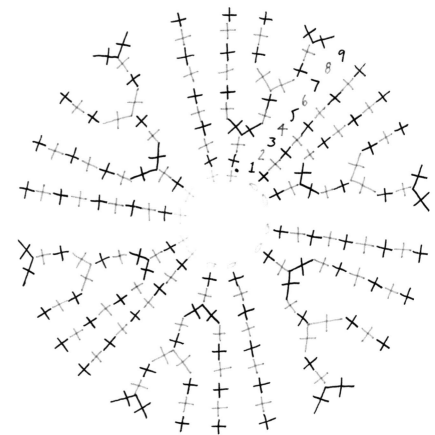

HIND LEGS CONTINUED
SHAPE THIGH
ROUNDS 1–9

HIND LEGS CONTINUED
SHAPE THIGH
ROUNDS 10–15

Rounds 10–11: 1 dc in each dc.

Round 12 (dec): (Dc2tog, 3 dc) 6 times (24 sts).

Stuff leg before continuing.

Round 13 (dec): (Dc2tog, 2 dc) 6 times (18 sts).

Round 14 (dec): (Dc2tog, 1 dc) 6 times (12 sts).

Round 15 (dec): (Dc2tog) 6 times (6 sts).

Break yarn and thread through last round of stitches. Pull tightly on end of yarn to close and fasten off, leaving a long tail of B at the end.

Tail

TIP

With 3.25mm hook and B, make a magic loop.

Round 1: 1 ch, 5 dc into loop (5 sts).

Round 2 (inc): (Dc2inc) 5 times (10 sts). Pull tightly on short end of yarn to close loop.

Round 3 (inc): (Dc2inc, 1 dc) 5 times (15 sts).

Rounds 4–5: 1 dc in each dc. Join A in last dc and carry unused yarn on WS of work.

STRIPES

The following is worked in rows.

Row 1 (RS): With A, 1 dc in each st with A, turn.

Row 2 (WS): 2 ch, 1 htr in next 3 dc, 1 dc in next 9 dc, 1 htr in next 3 dc, sl st to first htr, turn.

Rows 3–4: With B, rep rows 1–2.

Rows 5–16: Rep rows 1–4 3 times. Fasten off, leaving a long tail of B.

TAIL
TIP
ROUNDS 1–5

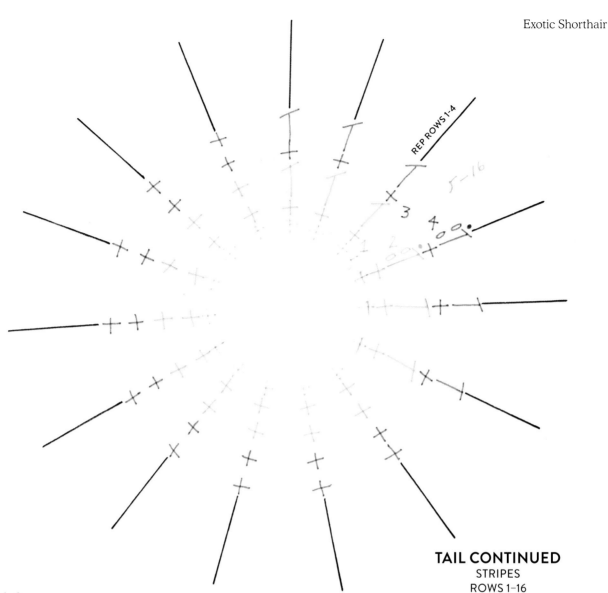

TAIL CONTINUED
STRIPES
ROWS 1–16

Making up

HEAD

Stuff the head. With the tails of yarn left after fastening off, sew the head in place. Stitch all around the neck edges. Insert more stuffing into the neck if necessary. Using three strands of embroidery thread, embroider the nose and the pupils of the eyes in satin stitch (see page 170). Work straight stitches around the pupils to form the irises (see page 170).

EARS

Stuff the ears lightly, keeping them flat. Sew the ears in place, near the back of the head, stitching all around the lower edges with the tails of yarn left after fastening off.

LEGS

Flatten the top of the legs and sew in place, stitching all around the top of the thighs with the tail of yarn left after fastening off.

TAIL

Stuff the tail. Sew the tail in place with the tail of yarn left after fastening off, positioning the joined edges of the rows at the back.

WHISKERS (OPTIONAL)

Attach three whiskers to the posts of the stitches on each side of the muzzle (see page 171). Trim the ends. Weave in all the yarn ends.

Calico Cat

THIS CALICO CAT USES SIMPLE COLOUR CHANGES TO CREATE THE PATCHED COAT. THE PATTERN CAN BE ADAPTED TO MAKE OTHER DOMESTIC SHORTHAIR CATS BY CHANGING THE COLOURS AND OMITTING THE PATCHES.

Materials

- Drops Lima, 65% wool, 35% alpaca (109yd/100m per 50g ball), or any DK yarn:
  1 x 50g ball in 1101 White (A)
- Drops Soft Tweed Mix, 50% wool, 25% alpaca, 25% viscose (142yd/130m per 50g ball), or any DK yarn:
  1 x 50g ball in 09 Raven (B)
  1 x 50g ball in 18 Carrot Cake (C)
- Stranded embroidery thread in green, such as DMC Stranded Cotton, shade 3364, for the eyes
- Metallic stranded embroidery thread in black, such as DMC Light Effects, shade E310, for the nose and pupils of the eyes
- 6 lengths of 0.3mm clear nylon thread, each measuring 4¾in (12cm), for the optional whiskers (not suitable for young children)
- 3.25mm (UK10:USD/3) crochet hook

- Blunt-ended yarn needle
- Toy stuffing

Size

- Approximately 4³/₈in (13.5cm) long, from tip of nose to back of hind legs
- Approximately 7¹/₈in (18cm) tall from top of head (excluding ears)

Tension

21 sts and 21 rows to 4in (10cm) over double crochet using 3.25mm hook. Use a larger or smaller hook if necessary to obtain the correct tension.

Method

The sitting calico cat's head, neck and body are worked in one piece, in rounds and rows of double crochet. Simple colour changes create the patches. The neck is worked along the edges of the rows that make up the top of the head and into the stitches at the underside of the muzzle. The shaping of the body is crocheted in short rows, working into just a few stitches of the previous row and then crocheting into an unworked stitch at the end of each subsequent row. Each ear is made up of two parts, the inner and outer ear. The outer ears are crocheted in different colours. The stitches of both pieces are crocheted into at the same time to join them together. The tail is crocheted using two colours in rows of double crochet and half treble stitches to form the curved shaping. The toes on the paws are made by crocheting bobbles that appear on the reverse side of the fabric. The thighs of the hind legs should be lightly stuffed so they have some flexibility and can easily bend into the sitting position. The eyes and nose are embroidered with stranded embroidery threads.

1 ch and 2 ch at beg of the row/round does not count as a st throughout.

Head and body

HEAD

Starting at front of muzzle, with 3.25mm hook and A, make a magic loop (see page 163).

Round 1: 1 ch, 6 dc into loop (6 sts).

Round 2 (inc): (Dc2inc) 6 times (12 sts). Pull tightly on short end to close loop.

Rounds 3–4: 1 dc in each dc. Turn at end of last round.

SHAPE FACE

The following is worked in rows.

Row 1 (WS) (inc): 1 ch, dc2inc, 1 dc in next dc, (1 dc, dc2inc) 3 times, (dc2inc, 1 dc) twice. Join B in last dc and carry unused yarn on WS of work, sl st to first dc, turn (18 sts).

Row 2 (RS): 1 dc in next 4 dc with B, 1 dc in next 4 dc with A. Join C in last dc. 1 dc in next 4 dc with C, 1 dc in next 6 dc with A, turn.

Row 3 (inc): 1 ch, 1 dc in next 6 dc with A; with C, 1 dc in next dc, (dc2inc, 1 dc) twice; with A, (dc2inc) twice; with B, (1 dc, dc2inc) twice, 1 dc in next dc, sl st to first dc, turn (24 sts).

COLOUR KEY FOR YARNS

FOR SHAPE FACE, TOP OF HEAD: ROWS 5–7, SHAPE BACK, SHAPE MIDDLE OF BODY, FRONT LEGS: ROUNDS 13–25, TAIL: ROWS 1–22

All other charts are shown in alternate rounds/rows of blue and black.

HEAD
ROUNDS 1–4

Row 4 (inc): With B, (1 dc, dc2inc, 1 dc) twice, 1 dc in next dc, dc2inc; with A, 1 dc in next 2 dc; with C, dc2inc, 1 dc in next dc, (1 dc, dc2inc, 1 dc) twice, finishing 6 sts before the end, turn (30 sts).

KEY

◎ MAGIC LOOP

⟋ CHAIN (CH)

• SLIP STITCH (SL ST)

┼ DOUBLE CROCHET (DC)

╳╳ DC2INC

⚹╳ DC3INC

╳╳ DC2TOG

⚹ DC6TOG

⊕ MAKE BOBBLE (MB)

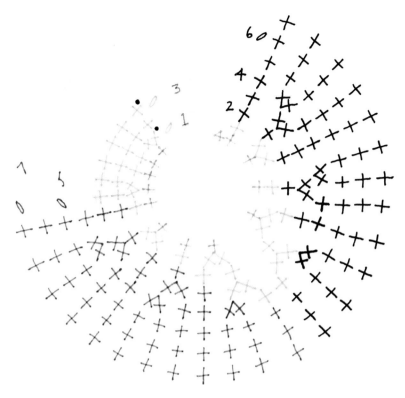

SHAPE FACE
ROWS 1–4
& TOP OF HEAD
ROWS 5–7

TOP OF HEAD

Row 5 (WS): 1 ch, 1 dc in next 12 dc with C, 1 dc in next 12 dc with B, turn.

Continue on these 24 sts.

Row 6 (RS): 1 ch, 1 dc in next 12 dc with B, 1 dc in next 12 dc with C, turn.

Row 7: Rep row 5.

Continue with B.

Rows 8–9: 1 ch, 1 dc in each dc to end, turn.

Row 10 (dec): 1 ch, (dc2tog, 2 dc) 6 times, turn (18 sts).

Row 11 (dec): 1 ch, (dc2tog, 1 dc) 6 times, turn (12 sts).

Row 12 (dec): 1 ch, (dc2tog) 6 times, turn (6 sts).

Row 13 (dec): 1 ch, dc6tog (insert the hook into the next st, yrh and draw back through the stitch 6 times (7 loops on hook), yrh and draw through all 7 loops on the hook, turn (1 st).

NECK

With A, work as for Siamese cat, page 69.

SHAPE FRONT OF BODY

With A, work as for Siamese cat,

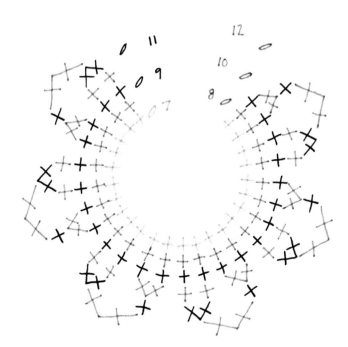

TOP OF HEAD CONTINUED
ROWS 8–12

TOP OF HEAD CONTINUED
ROW 13

93

SHAPE BACK

Row 1 (RS): 1 dc in next 2 dc, sl st in next dc, turn.

Row 2 (WS) (inc): With C, 1 dc in same st as sl st, 1 dc in next dc, (dc2inc) twice, 1 dc in next 2 dc, sl st in next dc, turn (32 sts).

Row 3 (inc): 1 dc in same st as sl st, 1 dc in next 3 dc, (dc2inc) twice, 1 dc in next 4 dc, sl st in next dc, turn (34 sts).

Row 4 (inc): 1 dc in same st as sl st, 1 dc in next 5 dc, (dc2inc) twice, 1 dc in next 6 dc, sl st in next dc, turn (36 sts).

Row 5 (inc): 1 dc in same st as sl st, 1 dc in next 7 dc, dc2inc; with B, dc2inc, 1 dc in next 8 dc, sl st in next dc, turn (38 sts).

Row 6 (inc): With B, 1 dc in same st as sl st, 1 dc in next 9 dc, dc2inc; with C, dc2inc, 1 dc in next 10 dc, sl st in next dc, turn (40 sts).

Row 7 (inc): With A, 1 dc in same st as sl st, 1 dc in next 11 dc, dc2inc; with B, dc2inc, 1 dc in next 12 dc, sl st in next dc, turn (42 sts).

Row 8 (inc): With B, 1 dc in same st as sl st, 1 dc in next 13 dc, dc2inc; with A, dc2inc, 1 dc in next 14 dc, sl st in next dc, turn (44 sts).
Continue with A.

Row 9 (inc): 1 dc in same st as sl st, 1 dc in next 15 dc, (dc2inc) twice, 1 dc in next 16 dc, sl st in next dc, turn (46 sts).

Row 10 (inc): 1 dc in same st as sl st, 1 dc in next 17 dc, (dc2inc) twice, 1 dc in next 18 dc, sl st in next dc, turn (48 sts).

Row 11: 1 dc in same st as sl st, 1 dc in next 41 dc, sl st in next dc, turn.

Row 12: 1 dc in same st as sl st, 1 dc in next 43 dc, sl st in next dc, turn.

Row 13: 1 dc in same st as sl st, 1 dc in next 45 dc, sl st in next dc, turn.

Row 14: 1 dc in same st as sl st, 1 dc in next 47 dc, sl st to first dc, turn.

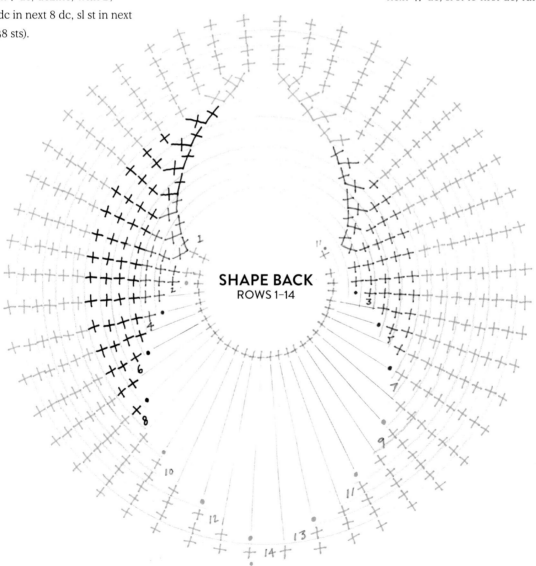

SHAPE BACK
ROWS 1–14

SHAPE MIDDLE
OF BODY
ROWS 1–10

SHAPE MIDDLE OF BODY

Row 1 (RS) (dec): 1 dc in next 4 dc, dc2tog, 1 dc in next 11 dc with A, 1 dc in next 14 dc with C, 1 dc in next 11 dc with A, dc2tog, 1 dc in next 4 dc, turn (46 sts).

Row 2 (WS) (dec): 1 ch, 1 dc in next 4 dc, dc2tog, 1 dc in next 10 dc with A, 1 dc in next 14 dc with C, 1 dc in next 10 dc with A, dc2tog, 1 dc in next 4 dc, sl st to first dc, turn (44 sts).

Row 3 (dec): 1 dc in next 4 dc, dc2tog, 1 dc in next 9 dc with A, 1 dc in next 14 dc with C, 1 dc in next 9 dc with A, dc2tog, 1 dc in next 4 dc, turn (42 sts).

Row 4 (dec): 1 ch, 1 dc in next 4 dc, dc2tog, 1 dc in next 8 dc with A, 1 dc in next 14 dc with C, 1 dc in next 8 dc with A, dc2tog, 1 dc in next 4 dc, sl st to first dc, turn (40 sts).

Row 5 (dec): 1 dc in next 4 dc, dc2tog, 1 dc in next 7 dc with A, 1 dc in next 14 dc with C, 1 dc in next 7 dc with A, dc2tog, 1 dc in next 4 dc, turn (38 sts).

Row 6 (dec): 1 ch, 1 dc in next 4 dc, dc2tog, 1 dc in next 6 dc with A, 1 dc in next 14 dc with C, 1 dc in next 6 dc with A, dc2tog, 1 dc in next 4 dc, sl st to first dc, turn (36 sts).

Row 7 (dec): 1 dc in next 4 dc, dc2tog, 1 dc in next 5 dc with A, 1 dc in next 14 dc with B, 1 dc in next 5 dc with A, dc2tog, 1 dc in next 4 dc, turn (34 sts).

Row 8 (dec): 1 ch, 1 dc in next 4 dc, dc2tog, 1 dc in next 4 dc with A, 1 dc in next 14 dc with B, 1 dc in next 4 dc with A, dc2tog, 1 dc in next 4 dc, sl st to first dc, turn (32 sts).

Row 9 (dec): 1 dc in next 4 dc, dc2tog, 1 dc in next 3 dc with A, 1 dc in next 14 dc with B, 1 dc in next 3 dc with A, dc2tog, 1 dc in next 4 dc, turn (30 sts).

Row 10: 1 ch, 1 dc in next 8 dc with A, 1 dc in next 14 dc with B, 1 dc in next 8 dc with A, sl st to first dc, turn.

SHAPE END OF BODY

Follow chart for the Siamese cat on page 73.

Continue with B.

The following is worked in rounds.

Round 1 (dec): (Dc2tog, 3 dc) 6 times (24 sts).

Stuff body before continuing.

Round 2 (dec): (Dc2tog, 2 dc) 6 times (18 sts).

Round 3 (dec): (Dc2tog, 1 dc) 6 times (12 sts).

Round 4 (dec): (Dc2tog) 6 times (6 sts).

Break yarn and thread through last 6 stitches. Pull tightly on end of yarn to close. Fasten off.

Ears

RIGHT EAR

With 3.25mm hook and A, make 4 ch.

Row 1: 1 dc in 2nd ch from hook, 1 dc in next ch, 3 dc in next ch, 1 dc in reverse side of next 2 ch, turn (7 sts).

Row 2 (inc): 1 ch, dc2inc, 1 dc in next 2 dc, dc3inc, 1 dc in next 2 dc, dc2inc (11 sts).

Fasten off, leaving a long tail of yarn. This completes the inner ear.

With C, make one more piece to match the first for the left outer ear. Turn work at the end and do not fasten off.

JOIN EAR PIECES

Place the two ear pieces together, with the inner ear facing up.

Next: 1 ch, inserting the hook under both loops of each stitch of the inner ear first, then the outer ear at the same time to join, dc2inc, 1 dc in next 4 dc, dc3inc, 1 dc in next 4 dc, dc2inc (15 sts). Fasten off, leaving a long tail of yarn.

LEFT EAR

Work as for right ear, using B to make the outer ear and joining the ear pieces.

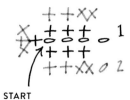

START

EARS
ROWS 1–2

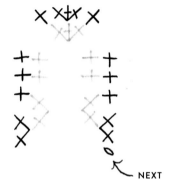

NEXT

JOIN EAR PIECES
INSERT HOOK INTO EACH STITCH
OF BOTH EAR PIECES AT SAME
TIME TO JOIN

Front legs

RIGHT LEG

Follow charts for rounds 1–12 of the black and white cat's front legs on pages 26–7.

The bobbles appear on the reverse side of the work. This will be the right side. See page 166 for instructions to make bobble (mb).

Starting at the base of the paw, with 3.25mm hook and A, make a magic loop.

Round 1 (WS): 1 ch, 6 dc into loop (6 sts).

Round 2 (inc): (Dc2inc) 6 times (12 sts). Pull tightly on short end of yarn to close loop.

Round 3 (inc): (Dc2inc, 2 dc) 4 times (16 sts).

Round 4: 1 dc in next 8 dc, (mb, 1 dc in next dc) 4 times, turn.

Round 5 (RS) (dec): 1 ch, 1 dc in first dc, (1 dc in next st, dc2tog) twice, 1 dc in next 9 dc (14 sts).

Round 6 (dec): (1 dc in next dc, dc2tog) twice, 1 dc in next 8 dc (12 sts).

Rounds 7–12: 1 dc in each dc.

Round 13 (inc): (Dc2inc, 3 dc) 3 times (15 sts).

Round 14: 1 dc in next 7 dc with A. Join C in last dc and carry unused yarn on WS of work. 1 dc in next 8 dc with C.

Rounds 15–17: 1 dc in next 7 dc with A, 1 dc in next 8 dc with C. Join B in last dc.

Round 18 (inc): (Dc2inc, 4 dc) twice with B, (dc2inc, 4 dc) once with C (18 sts).

Round 19: 1 dc in next 14 dc with B, 1 dc in next 4 dc with C. Continue with B.

Rounds 20–23: 1 dc in each dc. Stuff leg before continuing.

Round 24 (dec): (Dc2tog, 1 dc) 6 times (12 sts).

Round 25 (dec): (Dc2tog) 6 times (6 sts).

Break yarn and thread through last round of stitches. Pull tightly on end of yarn to close. Fasten off, leaving a long tail of B at the end.

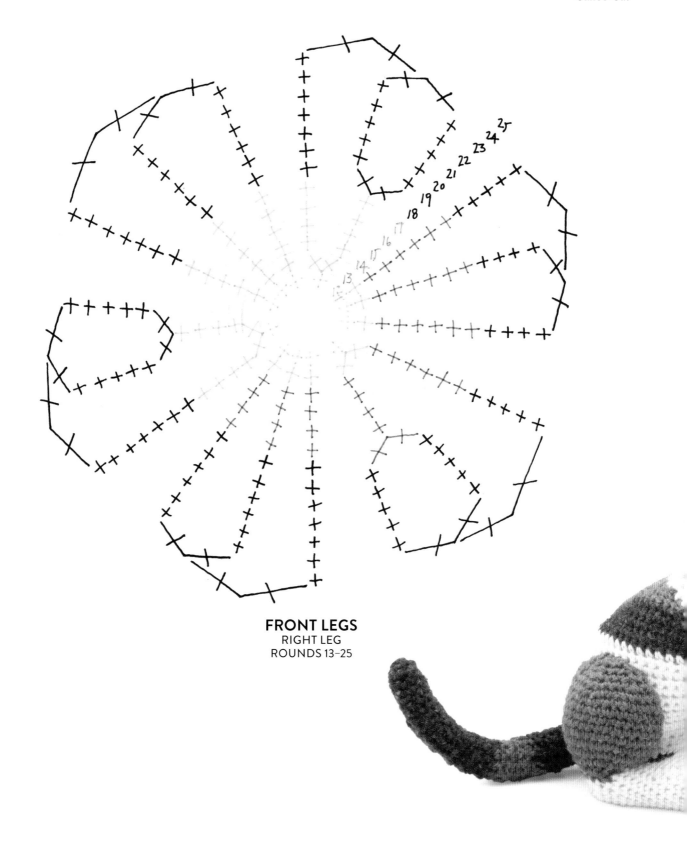

FRONT LEGS
RIGHT LEG
ROUNDS 13–25

13 14 15 16 17 18 19 20 21 22 23 24 25

LEFT LEG

Starting at the base of the paw, with 3.25mm hook and A, make a magic loop.

Rounds 1–12: Work as for rounds 1–12 of right leg.

Round 13 (inc): (Dc2inc, 3 dc) once with A. Join C in last dc and carry unused yarn on WS of work; (dc2inc, 3 dc) once with C, (dc2inc, 3 dc) once with A (15 sts).

Rounds 14–17: 1 dc in next 4 dc with A, 1 dc in next 8 dc with C, 1 dc in next 3 dc with A.

Round 18 (inc): (Dc2inc, 4 dc) once with A, (dc2inc, 4 dc) twice with C (18 sts).

Rounds 19–23: 1 dc in next 6 dc with A, 1 dc in next 12 dc with C. Stuff leg before continuing.

Round 24 (dec): (Dc2tog, 1 dc) twice with A, (dc2tog, 1 dc) 4 times with C (12 sts).

Round 25 (dec): (Dc2tog) 6 times with A (6 sts).

Break yarn and thread through last round of stitches. Pull tightly on end of yarn to close. Fasten off, leaving a long tail of A at the end.

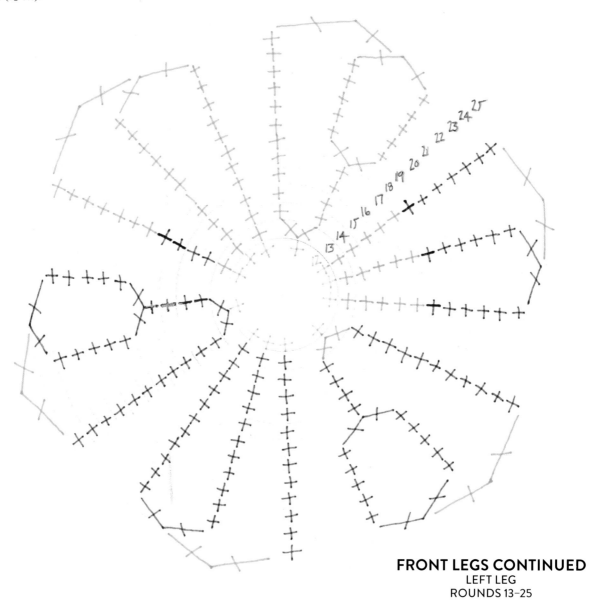

FRONT LEGS CONTINUED
LEFT LEG
ROUNDS 13–25

Hind legs

RIGHT LEG

Starting at the front of the paw, with 3.25mm hook and A, make 6 ch.

Round 1 (WS): 1 dc in 2nd ch from hook, (mb, 1 dc in next ch) twice, 1 dc in reverse side of each ch to end (10 sts).

Round 2 (inc): 1 dc in next dc, mb in same st as last dc, 1 dc in next dc, dc2inc, 1 dc in next dc, mb, 1 dc in same st as last st, (dc2inc, 1 dc) twice, dc2inc, turn (16 sts).

Round 3 (RS): 1 ch, 1 dc in each st.

Rounds 4–6: 1 dc in each dc.

Round 7 (dec): (1 dc, dc2tog, 1 dc) twice, 1 dc in next 8 dc (14 sts).

Round 8: 1 dc in each dc.

Round 9 (dec): Dc2tog, 1 dc in next 2 dc, dc2tog, 1 dc in next 8 dc (12 sts).

Rounds 10–14: 1 dc in each dc.

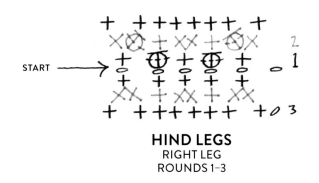

HIND LEGS
RIGHT LEG
ROUNDS 1–3

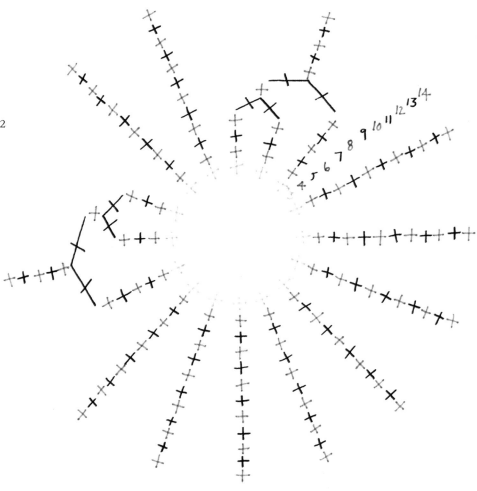

HIND LEGS CONTINUED
RIGHT LEG
ROUNDS 4–14

SHAPE BACK OF LEG

Round 15: 1 dc in next dc, ending at the side of the leg; 6 ch, skip the 6 dc at the front of the leg, 1 dc in next 5 dc.

Round 16: 1 dc in next dc, 1 dc in next 6 ch, 1 dc in next 5 dc.

Break yarn and thread through last round of stitches. Pull tightly on end of yarn to close and fasten off.

SHAPE RIGHT THIGH

With RS of leg facing, 3.25mm hook, join C with a sl st to first of 6 skipped dc of round 14.

Round 1: 1 dc in same st as sl st, 1 dc in next 5 dc, 1 dc in reverse side of next 6 ch (12 sts).

Round 2 (inc): (Dc2inc, 1 dc) 6 times (18 sts).

Round 3 (inc): (Dc2inc, 2 dc) 6 times (24 sts).

Round 4 (inc): (Dc2inc, 3 dc) 6 times (30 sts).

Rounds 5–11: 1 dc in each dc.

HIND LEGS CONTINUED
SHAPE BACK OF LEG
ROUNDS 15–16

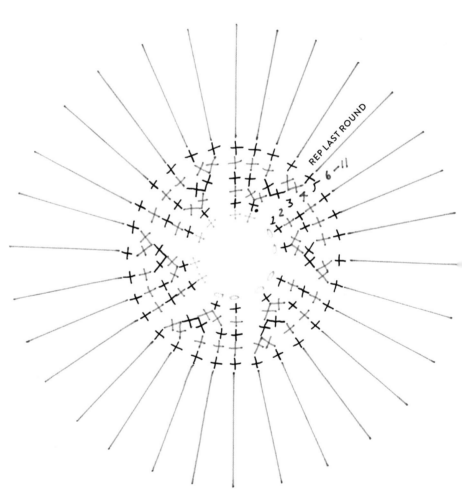

HIND LEGS CONTINUED
SHAPE RIGHT THIGH
ROUNDS 1–11

Round 12 (dec): (Dc2tog, 3 dc) 6 times (24 sts).

Stuff the paw and lightly stuff the thigh before continuing.

Round 13 (dec): (Dc2tog, 2 dc) 6 times (18 sts).

Round 14 (dec): (Dc2tog, 1 dc) 6 times (12 sts).

Round 15 (dec): (Dc2tog) 6 times (6 sts).

Break yarn and thread through last round of stitches. Pull tightly on end of yarn to close and fasten off, leaving a long tail of yarn.

LEFT LEG

Starting at the base of the paw, with 3.25mm hook and A, make 6 ch.

Rounds 1–16: Work as for rounds 1–16 of right hind leg.

SHAPE LEFT THIGH

With RS of leg facing, 3.25mm hook, and B, sl st in first of skipped 6 dc of round 14.

Rounds 1–15: Work as for rounds 1–15 of right thigh.

Break yarn and thread through last round of stitches. Pull tightly on end of yarn to close and fasten off, leaving a long tail of yarn.

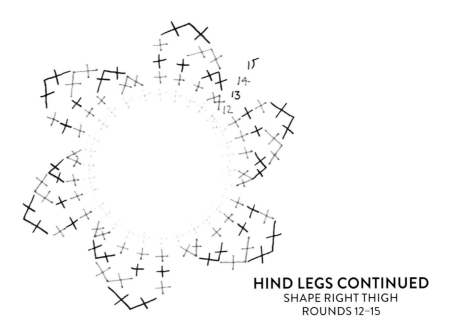

HIND LEGS CONTINUED
SHAPE RIGHT THIGH
ROUNDS 12–15

Tail

TIP

With 3.25mm hook and B, make a magic loop.

Round 1: 1 ch, 6 dc into loop (6 sts).

Round 2 (inc): (Dc2inc, 1 dc) 3 times (9 sts). Pull tightly on short end of yarn to close loop.

Rounds 3–7: 1 dc in each dc.

SHAPE TAIL

The following is worked in rows.

Row 1 (RS): 1 dc in each st, turn.

Row 2 (WS): 2 ch, 1 htr in next 2 dc, 1 dc in next 5 dc, 1 htr in next 2 dc, sl st to first htr, turn.

Row 3: 1 dc in next 7 sts. Join C in last dc and carry unused yarn on WS of work. 1 dc in next 2 sts with C, turn.

Row 4: With C, 2 ch, 1 htr in next 2 dc, 1 dc in next 2 dc; with B, 1 dc in next 3 dc, 1 htr in next 2 dc, sl st to first htr, turn.

Row 5: 1 dc in next 4 sts with B, 1 dc in next 5 sts with C, turn.

Row 6: With C, 2 ch, 1 htr in next 2 dc, 1 dc in next 3 dc; with B, 1 dc in next 2 dc, 1 htr in next 2 dc, sl st to first htr, turn.

Row 7: 1 dc in next 6 sts with B, 1 dc in next 3 sts with C, turn.

Row 8: With C, 2 ch, 1 htr in next 2 dc, 1 dc in next dc; with B, 1 dc in next 4 dc, 1 htr in next 2 dc, sl st to first htr, turn.

Rows 9–10: Rep rows 1—2 with B.

Row 11: 1 dc in next 3 sts with C, 1 dc in next 6 sts with B, turn.

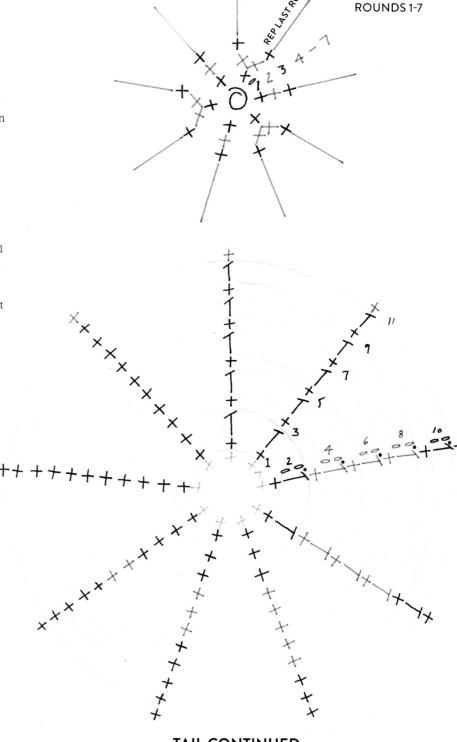

TAIL
TIP
ROUNDS 1-7

TAIL CONTINUED
SHAPE TAIL
ROWS 1–11

Row 12: With B, 2 ch, 1 htr in next 2 dc, 1 dc in next dc; with C, 1 dc in next 4 dc, 1 htr in next 2 dc, sl st to first htr, turn.

Row 13: 1 dc in next 6 sts with C, 1 dc in next 3 sts with B, turn.

Row 14: Rep row 12.

Row 15: 1 dc in next 4 sts with C, 1 dc in next 5 sts with B, turn.

Row 16: With B, 2 ch, 1 htr in next 2 dc, 1 dc in next 5 dc; with C, 1 htr in next 2 dc, sl st to first htr, turn.

Continue with B.

Rows 17–18: Rep rows 1–2.

Row 19: 1 dc in each dc, turn.

Row 20: 1 ch, 1 dc in each dc, sl st to first dc, turn.

Rows 21–22: Rep rows 19–20.

Fasten off, leaving a long tail of B.

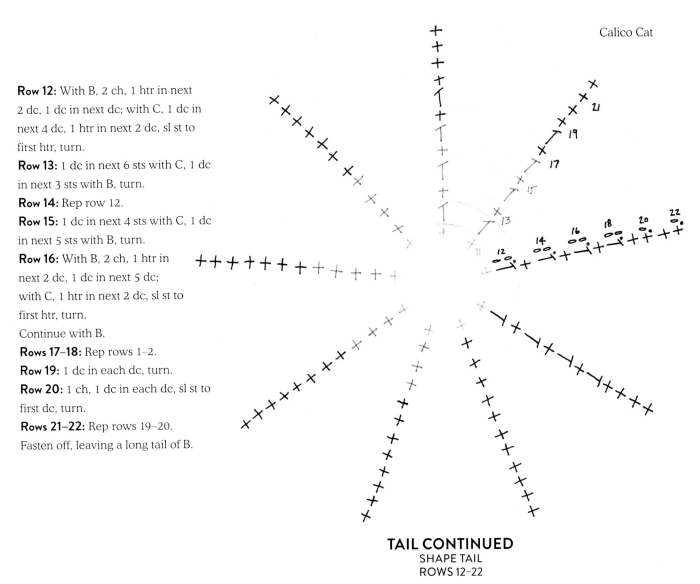

TAIL CONTINUED
SHAPE TAIL
ROWS 12–22

Making up

HEAD

Embroider the nose in satin stitch (see page 170) using three strands of metallic embroidery thread. With the thread used for the nose, embroider the pupils of the eyes. Work straight stitches around the pupils to form the irises (see page 170).

EARS

Stuff the ears lightly, keeping them flat. Sew the ears in place, near the back of the head, stitching all around the lower edges with the tails of yarn left after fastening off.

LEGS

Flatten the top of the legs and sew in place, stitching all around the top of the thighs with the tail of yarn left after fastening off.

TAIL

Stuff the tail. Sew the tail in place with the tail of yarn left after fastening off, positioning it so it curls up or wraps around the side of the body.

WHISKERS (OPTIONAL)

Attach three whiskers to the posts of the stitches on each side of the muzzle (see page 171). Trim the ends. Weave in all the yarn ends.

Ginger Cat

THIS IS A MORE INTRICATE PROJECT, INVOLVING SHORT ROWS AND COLOUR CHANGES. THE STRIPES CAN BE OMITTED TO MAKE A BICOLOUR CAT, SUCH AS A SLEEPING BLACK AND WHITE DOMESTIC SHORTHAIR.

Materials

- Scheepjes Softfun, 60% cotton, 40% acrylic (153yd/140m per 50g ball), or any DK yarn:
  1 x 50g ball in 2426 Lace(A)
  1 x 50g ball in 2466 Peach (B)
  1 x 50g ball in 2431 Clay (C)
- Stranded embroidery thread in black, such as Anchor Stranded Cotton, shade 0403, for the eyes
- Stranded embroidery thread in pink such as Anchor Stranded Cotton, shade 0893, for the nose
- 6 lengths of 0.3mm clear nylon thread, each measuring 4¾in (12cm), for the optional whiskers (not suitable for young children)
- 3.25mm (UK10:USD/3) crochet hook
- Blunt-ended yarn needle
- Toy stuffing

Size

- Approximately 6¼in (16cm) body length, from top of head to end of body

Tension

21 sts and 20 rows to 4in (10cm) over double crochet using 3.25mm hook. Use a larger or smaller hook if necessary to obtain the correct tension.

Method

The sleeping ginger cat's head and body are worked in one piece, in rounds and rows of double crochet. Three colours are used to create the white chin, chest, tummy and feet, and the striped tabby pattern. The first row of the body is worked into the stitches at the underside of the muzzle and along the edges of the rows that make up the top of the head. Short rows form the curled-up body shape, working into just a few stitches of the previous row and then crocheting into an unworked stitch at the end of each subsequent row. Each ear is made up of two identical crocheted parts that are worked in rows and joined by crocheting into each stitch of both pieces at the same time. The curl in the tail is created by using double crochet and half treble stitches, and the repeated pattern is worked in two colours. The toes on the paws are produced by crocheting bobbles that appear on the reverse side of the fabric. The body and tops of the legs should be stuffed lightly so as not to make the sleepy cat too bulky. The eyes, nose and paw pads are embroidered with stranded embroidery threads.

1 ch and 2 ch at beg of the row/round does not count as a st throughout.

Head and body

HEAD

Starting at front of muzzle, with 3.25mm hook and A, make a magic loop (see page 163).

Round 1: 1 ch, 6 dc into loop (6 sts).

Round 2 (inc): (Dc2inc) 6 times (12 sts). Pull tightly on short end to close loop.

Round 3: 1 dc in each dc, turn.

SHAPE FACE

The following is worked in rows.

Row 1 (WS): 1 ch, 1 dc in next 4 dc. Join B in last dc and carry unused yarn on WS of work. 1 dc in next 8 dc with B, sl st to first dc, turn.

Row 2 (RS) (inc): Dc2inc with B. Join C in last dc; 1 dc in next dc with C; with B, dc2inc, 1 dc in next 2 dc, dc2inc; with C, 1 dc in next dc; with B, dc2inc; with A, 1 dc in next dc, (dc2inc) twice, 1 dc in next dc, turn (18 sts).

Row 3 (inc): With A, 1 ch, 1 dc in next 6 dc; with B, dc2inc, 1 dc in next dc; dc2inc with C, (1 dc, dc2inc, 1 dc) twice with B, dc2inc with C; with B, 1 dc in next dc, dc2inc, sl st to first dc, turn (24 sts).

Row 4 (inc): Dc2inc, 1 dc in next dc with B, 1 dc in next 2 dc with C, (1 dc, dc2inc) twice with B, 1 dc in next 2 dc with C, (dc2inc, 1 dc) twice with B, 1 dc in next 2 dc with C; with B, 1 dc in next dc, dc2inc, finishing 6 sts before the end, turn (30 sts).

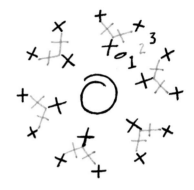

HEAD
ROUNDS 1–3

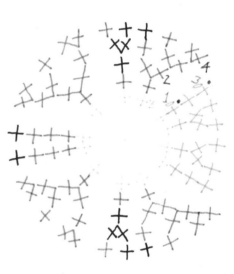

SHAPE FACE
ROWS 1–4

TOP OF HEAD

Row 5: 1 ch, (3 dc with B, 1 dc with C) twice, (1 dc with B, 1 dc with C) twice, (1 dc with C, 1 dc with B) twice, (1 dc with C, 3 dc with B) twice, turn.

Continue on these 24 sts.

Row 6: 1 ch, 1 dc in next 5 dc with B, 1 dc in next dc with C, 1 dc in next 3 dc with B, (1 dc with C, 1 dc with B, 1 dc with C) twice, 1 dc in next 3 dc with B, 1 dc in next dc with C, 1 dc in next 5 dc with B, turn.

Row 7: 1 ch, *1 dc in next 4 dc with B, 1 dc in next dc with C, 1 dc in next 4 dc with B*, 1 dc in next 6 dc with C; rep from * to *, turn.

Row 8: 1 ch, 1 dc in next 3 dc with B, 1 dc in next dc with C, 1 dc in next 7 dc with B, 1 dc in next 2 dc with C, 1 dc in next 7 dc with B, 1 dc in next dc with C, 1 dc in next 3 dc with B, turn.

Row 9: 1 ch, 1 dc in next 2 dc with B, 1 dc in next dc with C, 1 dc in next 8 dc with B, 1 dc in next 2 dc with C, 1 dc in next 8 dc with B, 1 dc in next dc with C, 1 dc in next 2 dc with B, turn.

Row 10 (dec): 1 ch, (1 dc, dc2tog, 1 dc) twice with C, (1 dc with B, dc2tog with C, 1 dc with B) twice, (1 dc, dc2tog, 1 dc) twice with C, turn (18 sts).

Row 11 (dec): 1 ch, *dc2tog with C; with B, 1 dc in next dc, dc2tog, 1 dc in next dc; dc2tog with C*, 1 dc in next 2 dc with B; rep from * to *, turn (12 sts).

Row 12 (dec): 1 ch, (dc2tog) twice with C, (dc2tog) twice with B, (dc2tog) twice with C (6 sts). Fasten off and thread C through last 6 stitches. Pull tightly on end of yarn and fasten off.

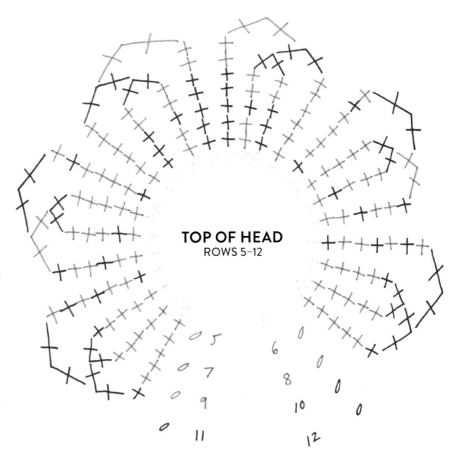

TOP OF HEAD
ROWS 5–12

KEY

∅ CHAIN (CH)

• SLIP STITCH (SL ST)

+ DOUBLE CROCHET (DC)

×× DC2INC

⁜× DC3INC

✕✕ DC2TOG

⊕ MAKE BOBBLE (MB)

(A) (B) (C)

COLOUR KEY FOR YARNS

FOR SHAPE FACE, TOP OF HEAD, SHAPE TOP OF BODY, SHAPE MIDDLE OF BODY, FRONT LEGS: SHAPE LEG, HIND LEGS: SHAPE RIGHT THIGH, TAIL STRIPES

All other charts are shown in alternate rounds/rows of blue and black.

SHAPE TOP OF BODY

With RS of head facing and 3.25mm hook, skip first 3 of unworked 6 dc of row 4 of shape face and join A with a sl st to next dc.

Row 1 (RS): 2 dc in same st as sl st, 1 dc in next dc, dc2inc, join B in last dc and work 7 dc evenly along edge of the rows of the first side of the head, joining C in the fourth st and working last 3 dc with C; work 7 dc evenly along edge of the rows of the other side of the head, changing to B for the last 4 dc; working in rem 3 unworked sts of round 8 of head with A, dc2inc, 1 dc in next dc, dc2inc, sl st to first dc, turn (24 sts).

Row 2 (WS): 1 dc in next 4 dc with A, 1 dc in next 5 dc with B, (1 dc with C, 1 dc with B, 1 dc with C) twice, 1 dc in next 5 dc with B, 1 dc in next 4 dc with A, turn.

Row 3 (inc): 1 ch, 1 dc in next dc, dc2inc, 1 dc in next 2 dc with A; with C, dc2inc, 1 dc in next 5 dc; with B, 1 dc in next dc, (dc2inc) twice with C, 1 dc in next dc with B, 1 dc in next 5 dc with C, dc2inc; with A, 1 dc in next 2 dc, dc2inc, 1 dc in next dc, sl st to first dc, turn (30 sts).

Row 4: 1 dc in next 5 dc with A, 1 dc in next 9 with B, 1 dc in next 2 dc with C, 1 dc in next dc with B, sl st in next dc, turn.

Row 5: 1 dc in same st as sl st, 1 dc in next dc with B, 1 dc in next 2 dc with C, 1 dc in next 2 dc with B, sl st in next dc, turn.

Row 6: 1 dc in same st as sl st, 1 dc in next 2 dc with B, 1 dc in next 2 dc with C, 1 dc in next 3 dc with B, sl st in next dc, turn.

Row 7 (inc): 1 dc in same st as sl st, 1 dc in next 3 dc with B, (dc2inc) twice with C, 1 dc in next 4 dc with B, sl st in next dc, turn (32 sts).

Row 8: 1 dc in same st as sl st, 1 dc in next 5 dc with C, 1 dc in next 2 dc with B, 1 dc in next 5 dc with C, 1 dc in next dc with B, sl st in next dc, turn.

Row 9: 1 dc in same st as sl st, (4 dc with B, 1 dc with C) twice, 1 dc in next 5 dc with B, sl st in next dc, turn.

Row 10: 1 dc in same st as sl st, 1 dc in next 5 dc with B, 1 dc in next dc with C, 1 dc in next 4 dc with B, 1 dc in next dc with C, 1 dc in next 6 dc with B, sl st in next dc, turn.

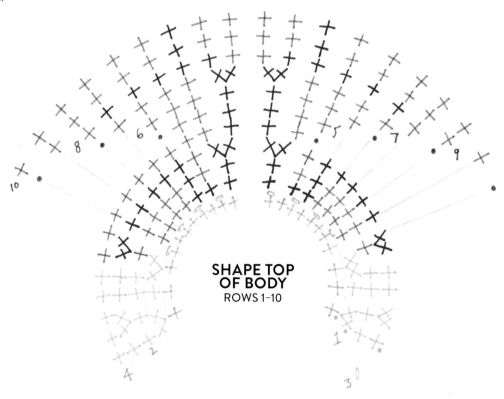

**SHAPE TOP
OF BODY**
ROWS 1–10

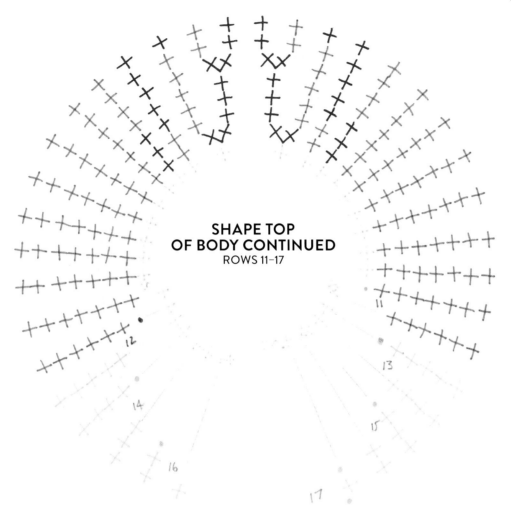

**SHAPE TOP
OF BODY CONTINUED**
ROWS 11–17

Row 11 (inc): 1 dc in same st as sl st, 1 dc in next 6 dc with B, 1 dc in next dc with C, 1 dc in next dc with B, (dc2inc) twice with C, 1 dc in next dc with B, 1 dc in next dc with C, 1 dc in next 7 dc with B, sl st in next dc, turn (34 sts).

Row 12: 1 dc in same st as sl st, 1 dc in next 7 dc with B, 1 dc in next dc with C, 1 dc in next 2 dc with B, 1 dc in next 2 dc with C, 1 dc in next 2 dc with B, 1 dc in next dc with C, 1 dc in next 8 dc with B, sl st in next dc with A, turn.

Row 13: 1 dc in same st as sl st with A, 1 dc in next 8 dc with B, (2 dc with C, 1 dc with B) twice, 1 dc in next 2 dc with C, 1 dc in next 8 dc with B, 1 dc in next dc with A, sl st in next dc, turn.

Row 14: 1 dc in same st as sl st, 1 dc in next dc with A, 1 dc in next 9 dc with B, (1 dc with C, 1 dc with B, 1 dc with C) twice, 1 dc in next 9 dc with B, 1 dc in next 2 dc with A, sl st in next dc, turn.

Row 15: 1 dc in same st as sl st, 1 dc in next 2 dc with A, 1 dc in next 9 dc with B, 1 dc in next dc with C, 1 dc in next dc with B, (dc2inc) twice with C, 1 dc in next dc with B, 1 dc in next dc with C, 1 dc in next 9 dc with B, 1 dc in next 3 dc with A, sl st in next dc, turn.

Row 16: 1 dc in same st as sl st, 1 dc in next 3 dc with A, 1 dc in next 9 dc with B, 1 dc in next dc with C, 1 dc in next 2 dc with B, 1 dc in next 2 dc with C, 1 dc in next 2 dc with B, 1 dc in next dc with C, 1 dc in next 9 dc with B, 1 dc in next 4 dc with A, sl st in next dc, turn.

Row 17: 1 dc in same st as sl st, 1 dc in next 4 dc with A, 1 dc in next 9 dc with B, (2 dc with C, 1 dc with B) twice, 1 dc in next 2 dc with C, 1 dc in next 9 dc with B, 1 dc in next 5 dc with A, sl st to first dc, turn.

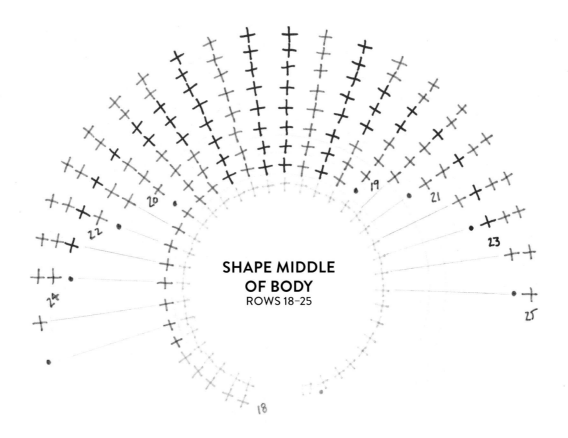

SHAPE MIDDLE OF BODY
ROWS 18–25

SHAPE MIDDLE OF BODY

Row 18: 1 dc in next 5 dc with A, 1 dc in next 10 dc with B, (1 dc with C, 1 dc with B, 1 dc with C) twice, 1 dc in next dc with B, sl st in next dc, turn.

Row 19: 1 dc in same st as sl st, 1 dc in next dc with B, (1 dc with C, 1 dc with B, 1 dc with C) twice, 1 dc in next 2 dc with B, sl st in next dc, turn.

Row 20: 1 dc in same st as sl st, 1 dc in next 2 dc with B, (1 dc with C, 1 dc with B, 1 dc with C) twice, 1 dc in next 3 dc with B, sl st in next dc, turn.

Row 21: 1 dc in same st as sl st, 1 dc in next 2 dc with B, (2 dc with C, 1 dc with B) 3 times, 1 dc in next 2 dc with B, sl st in next dc, turn.

Row 22: 1 dc in same st as sl st, 1 dc in next 2 dc with B, 1 dc in next 3 dc with C, 1 dc in next dc with B, 1 dc in next 2 dc with C, 1 dc in next dc with B, 1 dc in next 3 dc with C, 1 dc in next 3 dc with B, sl st in next dc with C, turn.

Row 23: 1 dc in same st as sl st, 1 dc in next 6 dc with C, 1 dc in next dc with B, 1 dc in next 2 dc with C, 1 dc in next dc with B, 1 dc in next 7 dc with C, sl st in next dc with B, turn.

Row 24: 1 dc in same st as sl st, 1 dc in next 6 dc with B, (1 dc with C, 1 dc with B, 1 dc with C) twice, 1 dc in next 7 dc with B, sl st in next dc, turn.

Row 25: 1 dc in same st as sl st, 1 dc in next 7 dc with B, (1 dc with C, 1 dc with B, 1 dc with C) twice, 1 dc in next 8 dc with B, sl st in next dc, turn.

Row 26: 1 dc in same st as sl st with B, 1 dc in next 4 dc with C, 1 dc in next 4 dc with B, (1 dc with C, 1 dc with B, 1 dc with C) twice, 1 dc in next 4 dc with B, 1 dc in next 4 dc with C, 1 dc in next dc with B, sl st in next dc, turn.

Row 27: 1 dc in same st as sl st, 1 dc in next 4 dc with B, 1 dc in next 3 dc

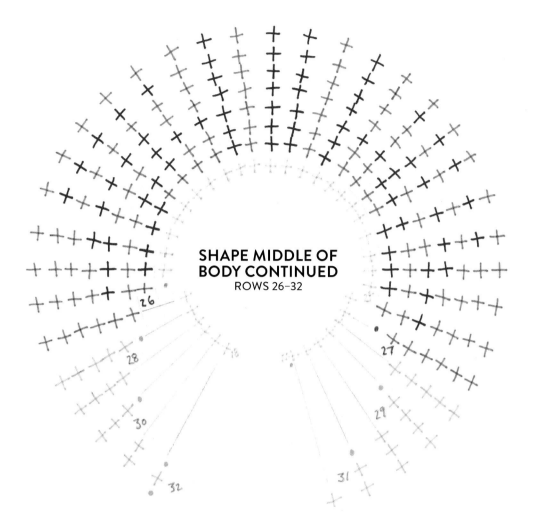

**SHAPE MIDDLE OF
BODY CONTINUED**
ROWS 26–32

with C, 1 dc in next 2 dc with B, (1 dc with C, 1 dc with B, 1 dc with C) twice, 1 dc in next 2 dc with B, 1 dc in next 3 dc with C, 1 dc in next 5 dc with B, sl st in next dc with A, turn.

Row 28: 1 dc in same st as sl st with A, 1 dc in next dc with B, 1 dc in next 3 dc with C, 1 dc in next 3 dc with B, 1 dc in next 4 dc with C, 1 dc in next dc with B, 1 dc in next 2 dc with C, 1 dc in next dc with B, 1 dc in next 4 dc with C, 1 dc in next 3 dc with B, 1 dc in next 3 dc with C, 1 dc in next dc with B, 1 dc in next dc with A, sl st in next dc, turn.

Row 29: 1 dc in same st as sl st, 1 dc in next dc with A, 1 dc in next 3 dc with B, 1 dc in next 5 dc with C, 1 dc in next 2 dc with B, (1 dc with C, 1 dc with B, 1 dc with C) twice, 1 dc in next 2 dc with B, 1 dc in next 5 dc with C, 1 dc in next 3 dc with B, 1 dc in next 2 dc with A, sl st in next dc, turn.

Row 30: 1 dc in same st as sl st, 1 dc in next 2 dc with A, 1 dc in next 10 dc with B, (1 dc with C, 1 dc with B, 1 dc with C) twice, 1 dc in next 10 dc with B, 1 dc in next 3 dc with A, sl st in next dc, turn.

Row 31: 1 dc in same st as sl st, 1 dc in next 3 dc with A, 1 dc in next 4 dc with B, 1 dc in next 5 dc with C, 1 dc in next dc with B, (1 dc with C, 1 dc with B, 1 dc with C) twice, 1 dc in next dc with B, 1 dc in next 5 dc with C, 1 dc in next 4 dc with B, 1 dc in next 4 dc with A, sl st in next dc, turn.

Row 32: 1 dc in same st as sl st, 1 dc in next 4 dc with A, 1 dc in next 10 dc with B, (1 dc with C, 1 dc with B, 1 dc with C) twice, 1 dc in next 10 dc with B, 1 dc in next 5 dc with A, sl st to first dc, turn.

111

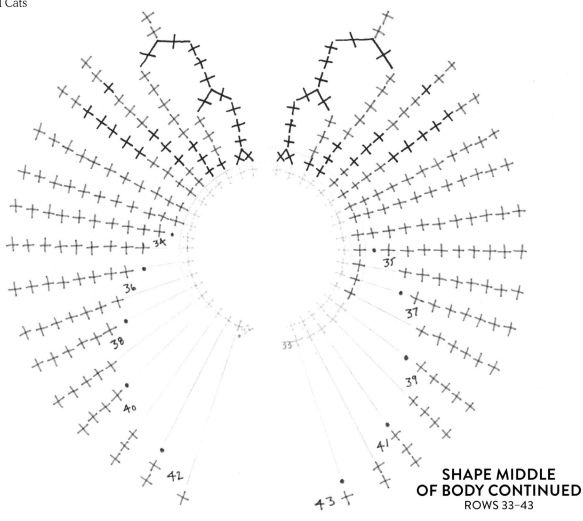

**SHAPE MIDDLE
OF BODY CONTINUED**
ROWS 33–43

Row 33 (dec): 1 dc in next 5 dc with A, 1 dc in next 9 dc with B, 1 dc in next 2 dc with C, (dc2tog) twice, 1 dc in next 2 dc; with B, 1 dc in next 4 dc, sl st in next dc, turn (34 sts).

Row 34: 1 dc in same st as sl st, 1 dc in next 4 dc with B, (1 dc with C, 1 dc with B, 1 dc with C) twice, 1 dc in next 5 dc with B, sl st in next dc, turn.

Row 35: 1 dc in same st as sl st, 1 dc in next 4 dc with B, (2 dc with C, 1 dc with B) 3 times, 1 dc in next 4 dc with B, sl st in next dc, turn.

Row 36: 1 dc in same st as sl st, 1 dc in next 5 dc with B, (1 dc with C, 2 dc with B, 1 dc with C) twice, 1 dc in

next 6 dc with B, sl st in next dc, turn.

Row 37 (dec): 1 dc in same st as sl st, 1 dc in next 5 dc with B, 1 dc in next 2 dc with C, 1 dc in next dc with B, (dc2tog) twice with C, 1 dc in next dc with B, 1 dc in next 2 dc with C, 1 dc in next 6 dc with B, sl st in next dc, turn (32 sts).

Row 38: 1 dc in same st as sl st, 1 dc in next 6 dc with B, (1 dc with C, 2 dc with B, 1 dc with C) twice, 1 dc in next 7 dc with B, sl st in next dc, turn.

Row 39: 1 dc in same st as sl st, 1 dc in next 7 dc with B, (1 dc with C, 2 dc with B, 1 dc with C) twice, 1 dc in next 8 dc with B, sl st in next dc, turn.

Row 40: 1 dc in same st as sl st, 1 dc in next 8 dc with B, (1 dc with C, 2 dc with B, 1 dc with C) twice, 1 dc in next 9 dc with B, sl st in next dc, turn.

Row 41 (dec): 1 dc in same st as sl st, 1 dc in next 9 dc with B, 1 dc in next 2 dc with C, (dc2tog) twice, 1 dc in next 2 dc; with B, 1 dc in next 10 dc, sl st in next dc, turn (30 sts).

Continue with B.

Row 42: 1 dc in same st as sl st, 1 dc in next 27 dc, sl st in next dc, turn.

Row 43: 1 dc in same st as sl st, 1 dc in next 29 dc. Do not turn.

Stuff the head and lightly stuff the body before continuing.

SHAPE END OF BODY

The following is worked in rounds.

Round 1 (dec): (Dc2tog, 3 dc) 6 times (24 sts).

Round 2 (dec): (Dc2tog, 2 dc) 6 times (18 sts).

Round 3 (dec): (Dc2tog, 1 dc) 6 times (12 sts).

Round 4 (dec): (Dc2tog) 6 times (6 sts).

Break yarn and thread through last 6 stitches. Pull tightly on end of yarn to close. Fasten off.

Ears (make 2)

With 3.25mm hook and A, make 4 ch.

Row 1: 1 dc in 2nd ch from hook, 1 dc in next ch, 3 dc in next ch, 1 dc in reverse side of next 2 ch, turn (7 sts).

Row 2 (inc): 1 ch, dc2inc, 1 dc in next 2 dc, dc3inc, 1 dc in next 2 dc, dc2inc (11 sts).

Fasten off, leaving a long tail of yarn. This completes the inner ear.

With B, make one more piece to match the first for the outer ear. Turn work at the end and do not fasten off.

JOIN EAR PIECES

Place the two ear pieces together, with the inner ear facing up.

Next: 1 ch, inserting the hook under both loops of each stitch of the inner ear first, then the outer ear at the same time to join, dc2inc, 1 dc in next 4 dc, dc3inc, 1 dc in next 4 dc, dc2inc (15 sts). Fasten off, leaving a long tail of yarn.

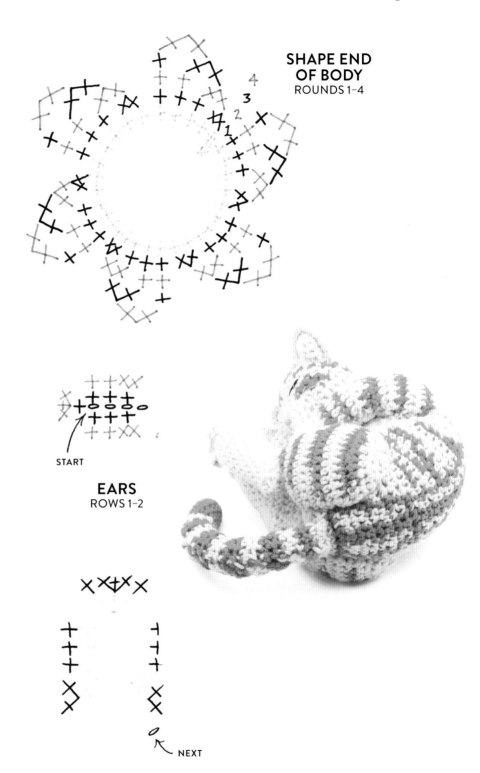

SHAPE END OF BODY
ROUNDS 1–4

EARS
ROWS 1–2

START

NEXT

JOIN EAR PIECES
INSERT HOOK INTO EACH STITCH OF BOTH EAR PIECES AT SAME TIME TO JOIN

Front legs (make 2)

PAW

The bobbles appear on the reverse side of the work. This will be the right side. See page 166 for instructions to make bobble (mb).

Starting at the front of the paw, with 3.25mm hook and A, make 6 ch.

Round 1 (WS): 1 dc in 2nd ch from hook, (mb, 1 dc in next ch) twice, 1 dc in reverse side of each ch to end (10 sts).

Round 2 (inc): 1 dc in next dc, mb in same st as last dc, 1 dc in next dc, dc2inc, 1 dc in next dc, mb, 1 dc in same st as last st, (dc2inc, 1 dc) twice, dc2inc, turn (16 sts).

Round 3 (RS): 1 ch, 1 dc in each st.

Round 4: 1 dc in each dc.

Round 5 (dec): (1 dc, dc2tog, 1 dc) twice, 1 dc in next 8 dc (14 sts).

Round 6 (dec): Dc2tog, 1 dc in next 2 dc, dc2tog, 1 dc in next 8 dc (12 sts).

Round 7: 1 dc in each dc. Join B in last dc and carry unused yarn on WS of work.

SHAPE LEG

The following is worked in rows.

Row 1 (RS): 1 dc in each dc with B, turn.

Row 2 (WS): 1 ch, 1 dc in next 6 dc. Join C in last dc and work 1 dc in next 6 dc with C, turn.

Row 3: 1 ch, 1 dc in each dc with B, turn.

Row 4: 1 ch, 1 dc in next 6 dc with B, 1 dc in next 6 dc with C, turn.

Rows 5–6: 1 ch, 1 dc in each dc with B, turn.

Row 7: 1 ch, (2 dc with C, 2 dc with B) twice, 1 dc in next 4 dc with B, turn.

Row 8: 1 ch, 1 dc in next 6 dc with B, 1 dc in next 6 dc with C, turn.

Row 9 (inc): 1 ch, (dc2inc, 3 dc) 3 times with B, turn (15 sts).

Row 10: 1 ch, 1 dc in each dc with B, turn.

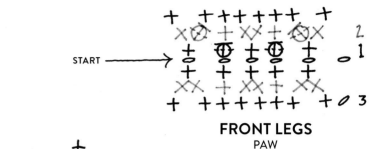

FRONT LEGS
PAW
ROUNDS 1–3

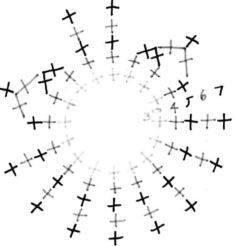

FRONT LEGS CONTINUED
PAW
ROUNDS 4–7

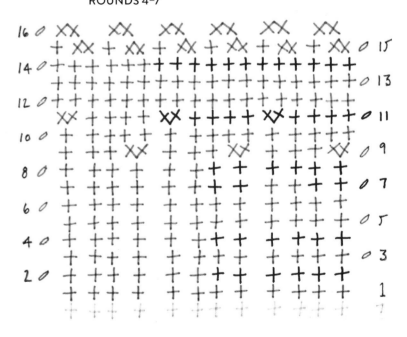

FRONT LEGS CONTINUED
SHAPE LEG
ROWS 1–16

Row 11 (inc): 1 ch, (4 dc, dc2inc) twice with C, (4 dc, dc2inc) once with B, turn (18 sts).

Rows 12–13: 1 ch, 1 dc in each dc with B, turn.

Row 14: 1 ch, 1 dc in next 6 dc with B, 1 dc in next 12 dc with C, turn. Continue with B.

Row 15 (dec): 1 ch, (dc2tog, 1 dc) 6 times, turn (12 sts).

Row 16 (dec): 1 ch, (dc2tog) 6 times (6 sts).

Fasten off, leaving a long tail of B at the end.

Hind legs

RIGHT LEG

Work rounds 1–16 as for the calico cat, pages 99–100.

SHAPE RIGHT THIGH

With RS of leg facing, 3.25mm hook, join B with a sl st to first of 6 skipped dc of round 14.

Row 1: 1 dc in same st as sl st, 1 dc in next 5 dc, 1 dc in reverse side of next 6 ch, turn (12 sts).

Row 2 (inc): 1 ch, (dc2inc, 1 dc) twice. Join C in last dc and carry unused yarn on WS of work, (dc2inc, 1 dc) twice with C, (dc2inc, 1 dc) twice with B, turn (18 sts).

Row 3 (inc): 1 ch, (dc2inc, 2 dc) 6 times with B, turn (24 sts).

Row 4 (inc): 1 ch, (dc2inc, 3 dc) twice with B, (dc2inc, 3 dc) twice with C, (dc2inc, 3 dc) twice with B, turn (30 sts).

Rows 5–6: 1 ch, 1 dc in each dc with B, turn.

Row 7: 1 ch, 1 dc in next 12 dc with B, 1 dc in next 6 dc with C, 1 dc in next 12 dc with B, turn.

Row 8: 1 ch, 1 dc in next 9 dc with B, 1 dc in next 12 dc with C, 1 dc in next 9 dc with B, turn.

Rows 9–10: 1 ch, 1 dc in each dc with B, turn.

Row 11: 1 ch, 1 dc in next 8 dc with B, 1 dc in next 14 dc with C, 1 dc in next 8 dc with B, turn.

Row 12 (dec): 1 ch, (dc2tog, 3 dc) twice with B, (dc2tog, 3 dc) twice with C, (dc2tog, 3 dc) twice with B, turn (24 sts). Continue with B.

Row 13 (dec): 1 ch, (dc2tog, 2 dc) 6 times, turn (18 sts).

Row 14 (dec): 1 ch, (dc2tog, 1 dc) 6 times, turn (12 sts).

Row 15 (dec): 1 ch (dc2tog) 6 times (6 sts).

Break yarn and thread through last round of stitches. Pull tightly on end of yarn to close and fasten off, leaving a long tail of B.

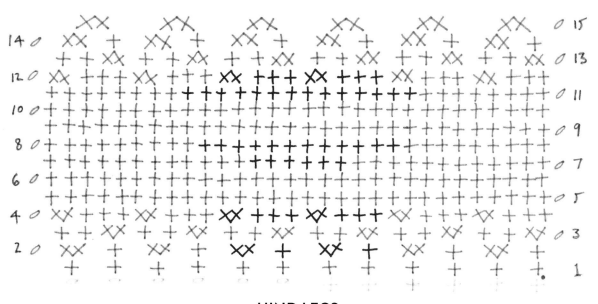

HIND LEGS
SHAPE RIGHT THIGH
ROWS 1–15

LEFT LEG

Work rounds 1–16 as for the calico cat's right leg, pages 99–100.

SHAPE LEFT THIGH

With RS of leg facing, 3.25mm hook, and B, sl st in reverse side of first of 6 ch of round 15.

Row 1: 1 dc in same st as sl st, 1 dc in next 5 ch, 1 dc in next 6 unworked dc of round 14, turn (12 sts).

Rows 2–15: Work as for rows 2–15 of right thigh.

Break yarn and thread through last round of stitches. Pull tightly on end of yarn to close and fasten off, leaving a long tail of B.

Tail

TIP

With 3.25mm hook and C, make a magic loop.

Round 1: 1 ch, 6 dc into loop (6 sts).

Round 2 (inc): (Dc2inc, 1 dc) 3 times (9 sts). Pull tightly on short end of yarn to close loop.

Rounds 3–7: 1 dc in each dc. Join B in last dc and carry unused yarn on WS of work.

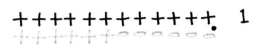

HIND LEGS CONTINUED
SHAPE LEFT THIGH
ROW 1

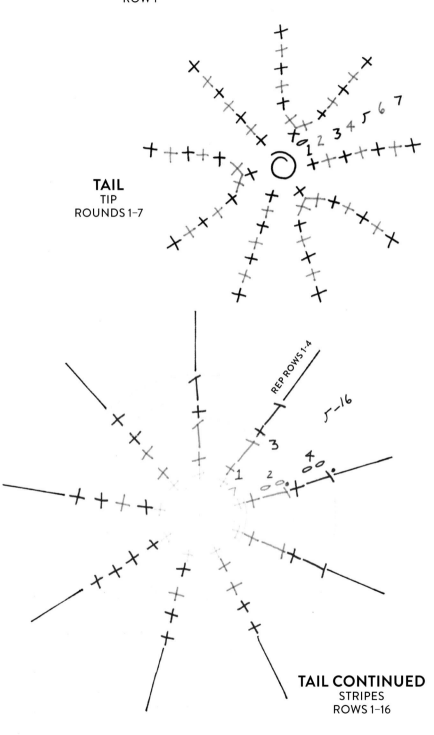

TAIL
TIP
ROUNDS 1–7

TAIL CONTINUED
STRIPES
ROWS 1–16

STRIPES

The following is worked in rows.

Row 1 (RS): 1 dc in next 3 dc with B, 1 dc in next 3 dc with C, 1 dc in next 3 dc with B, turn.

Row 2 (WS): With B, 2 ch, 1 htr in next 2 dc, 1 dc in next 2 dc; with C, 1 dc in next dc; with B, 1 dc in next 2 dc, 1 htr in next 2 dc, sl st to first htr, turn.

Row 3: 1 dc in each st with C, turn.

Row 4: With C, 2 ch, 1 htr in next 2 dc, 1 dc in next 5 dc, 1 htr in next 2 dc, sl st to first htr, turn.

Rows 5–16: Rep rows 1–4 3 times.

Row 17: Rep row 1.

Row 18: 1 ch, 1 dc in next 4 dc with B, 1 dc in next dc with C, 1 dc in next 4 dc with B, sl st to first dc, turn.

Row 19: 1 dc in each dc with C, turn.

Row 20: 1 ch, 1 dc in each dc with C, sl st to first dc, turn.

Rows 21–22: Rep rows 17–18.

Fasten off, leaving a long tail of B.

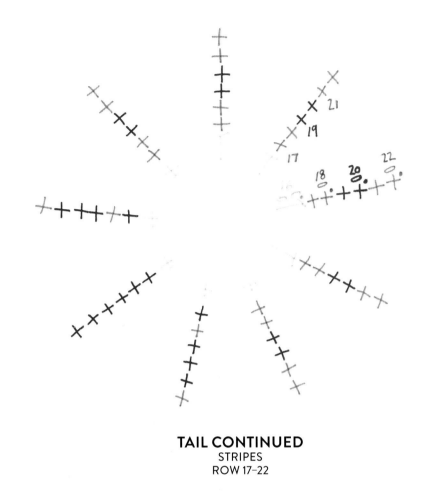

TAIL CONTINUED
STRIPES
ROW 17–22

Making up

HEAD

Embroider the nose in satin stitch (see page 170) using three strands of embroidery thread. With two strands of thread, embroider two straight stitches for each eye (see page 170).

EARS

Stuff the ears lightly, keeping them flat. Sew the ears in place, near the back of the head, stitching all around the lower edges with the tails of yarn left after fastening off.

LEGS

Thread tail of yarn through last row of stitches. Pull tightly on end of yarn to close. Sew the edges of the leg together, matching the rows, stuffing the paw and lightly stuffing the thigh as you sew. Embroider the paw pads in satin stitch using three strands of embroidery thread. Flatten the top of each leg. The seams of the hind legs should run down the centre of the inside leg, which will be placed against the body. The seams of the front legs will run down one side.

Sew the legs to the body, stitching all around the top of the thighs.

TAIL

Flatten the top of the tail and sew the edges together. Sew the tail to the end of the body.

WHISKERS (OPTIONAL)

Attach three whiskers to the posts of the stitches on each side of the muzzle (see page 171). Trim the ends.
Weave in all the yarn ends.

Ragdoll

LOOP STITCH IS USED TO CREATE THE COAT OF THE RAGDOLL CAT, WHOSE SOFT, SILKY FUR MAKES IT APPEAR BIGGER THAN IT ACTUALLY IS.

Materials

- Drops Puna, 100% alpaca (120yd/110m per 50g ball), or any DK yarn:
  2 x 50g balls in 01 Off White (A)
  2 x 50g balls in 06 Grey (B)
- Stranded embroidery thread in blue, such as Anchor Stranded Cotton, shade 0161, for the eyes
- Stranded embroidery thread in black, such as Anchor Stranded Cotton, shade 0403, for the pupils
- Stranded embroidery thread in pink, such as Anchor Stranded Cotton, shade 049, for the nose
- 6 lengths of 0.3mm clear nylon thread, each measuring 4¾in (12cm), for the optional whiskers (not suitable for young children)
- 3.25mm (UK10:USD/3) crochet hook
- Blunt-ended yarn needle
- Toy stuffing

Size

- Approximately 6⅞in (17.5cm) body length, from tip of nose to back of hind legs
- Approximately 6½in (16.5cm) tall from top of head (excluding ears)

Tension

22 sts and 26 rows to 4in (10cm) over double crochet using 3.25mm hook. Use a larger or smaller hook if necessary to obtain the correct tension.

Method

The cat's head, body and legs are worked in rounds and rows of double crochet and loop stitch. Sections on the body where the legs are to be placed are worked in double crochet only, and any loop stitches that will be covered by the head, legs and tail are simply tucked underneath when sewing the pieces together. Crocheted bobbles form the toes on the paws. The bobbles and loop stitches appear on the reverse side of the fabric. The neck is worked in rounds, starting by crocheting into the stitches at the underside of the muzzle, and then along the edges of the rows that make up the top of the head. A ruff of loop stitches is crocheted separately, slipped over the head and sewn in place. The tail is crocheted in alternate rows of double crochet and loop stitch. The edges of the last row are sewn together and the tail is stuffed lightly. The ears are worked in rows. Each ear is made up of two crocheted parts that are joined by crocheting into each stitch of both pieces at the same time. Lengths of yarn are threaded through the face, near the edges of the ruff, and attached to the ears and between the toes to form the tufty fur. The eyes and nose are embroidered with embroidery threads.

1 ch and 2 ch at beg of the row/round does not count as a st throughout.

Head

Starting at front of muzzle, with 3.25mm hook and A, make a magic loop (see page 163).

Round 1: 1 ch, 6 dc into loop (6 sts).
Round 2 (inc): (Dc2inc) 6 times (12 sts). Pull tightly on short end of yarn to close loop.
Rounds 3–4: 1 dc in each dc.

HEAD
ROUNDS 1–4

KEY

⊙ MAGIC LOOP

⌀ CHAIN (CH)

• SLIP STITCH (SL ST)

+ DOUBLE CROCHET (DC)

✕✕ DC2INC

⋆✕✕ DC3INC

✕✕ DC2TOG

⊕ MAKE BOBBLE (MB)

♀✕ LOOP STITCH (LP ST)

SHAPE FACE

The following is worked in rows.

Row 1 (RS) (inc): Dc2inc, 1 dc in next 2 dc, dc2inc. Join B in last dc and carry unused yarn on WS of work. *With B, 1 dc in next dc, dc2inc, 1 dc in next dc*; with A, (dc2inc) twice, rep from * to *, turn (18 sts).
Row 2 (WS): 1 ch, 1 dc in next 4 dc with B, 1 dc in next 4 dc with A, 1 dc in next 4 dc with B, 1 dc in next 6 dc with A, sl st to first dc, turn.
Row 3 (RS) (inc): 1 dc in next 6 dc with A; with B, 1 dc in next dc, (dc2inc, 1 dc) twice, (dc2inc) twice with A; with B, (1 dc, dc2inc) twice, 1 dc in next dc, turn (24 sts).
Row 4 (inc): With B, 1 ch, (1 dc, dc2inc, 1 dc) twice, 1 dc in next dc, dc2inc; with A, 1 dc in next 2 dc; with B, dc2inc, 1 dc in next dc, (1 dc, dc2inc, 1 dc) twice, finishing 6 sts before the end, turn (30 sts).

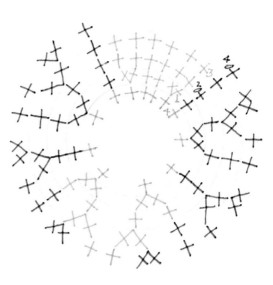

SHAPE FACE
ROWS 1–4

TOP OF HEAD

Continue with B.

Row 5 (WS): 1 ch, 1 dc in next 24 dc, turn.

Continue on these 24 sts.

Row 6 (RS): 1 ch, 1 dc in each dc, turn.

Rows 7–9: Rep last row.

Row 10 (dec): 1 ch, (dc2tog, 2 dc) 6 times, turn (18 sts).

Row 11 (dec): 1 ch, (dc2tog, 1 dc) 6 times, turn (12 sts).

Row 12 (dec): 1 ch, (dc2tog) 6 times (6 sts).

Fasten off and thread B through last 6 stitches. Pull tightly on end of yarn and fasten off.

NECK

With RS of head facing, 3.25mm hook and B, sl st to first of unworked 6 dc of row 3 of shape face.

Round 1: 1 dc in same st as sl st, 1 dc in next 5 dc, work 14 dc evenly along edge of the rows of head (20 sts).

Round 2 (inc): (Dc2inc, 4 dc) 4 times (24 sts).

Rounds 3–4: 1 dc in each dc.

Round 5: 1 dc in next 8 dc, sl st to first dc and fasten off, leaving a long tail of yarn.

COLOUR KEY FOR YARNS

FOR SHAPE FACE & SHAPE MIDDLE OF BODY: ROWS 8–21

All other charts are shown in alternate rounds/rows of blue and black.

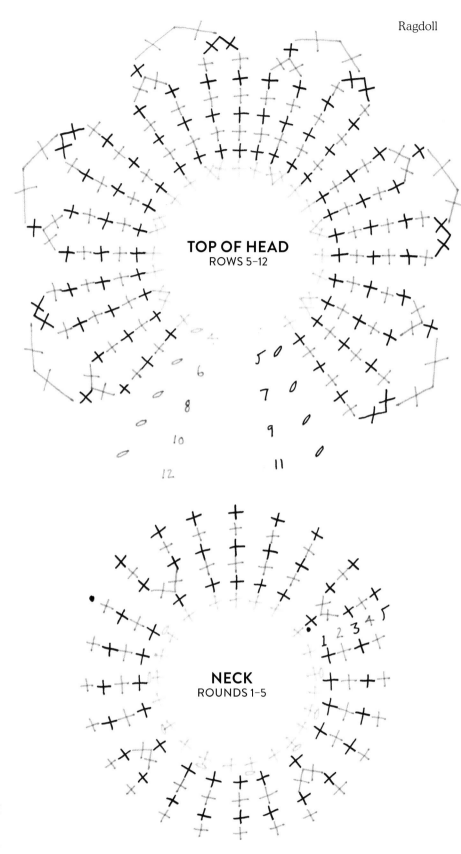

TOP OF HEAD
ROWS 5–12

NECK
ROUNDS 1–5

Ears (make 2)

With 3.25mm hook and A, make 4 ch.

Row 1: 1 dc in 2nd ch from hook, 1 dc in next ch, 3 dc in next ch, 1 dc in reverse side of next 2 ch, turn (7 sts).

Row 2 (inc): 1 ch, dc2inc, 1 dc in next 2 dc, dc3inc, 1 dc in next 2 dc, dc2inc (11 sts).

Fasten off, leaving a long tail of yarn. This completes the inner ear.

With B, make one more piece to match the first for the outer ear. Turn work at the end and do not fasten off.

Body

The loops appear on the reverse side of the work. This will be the right side. See page 166 for instructions on loop stitch (lp st).

SHAPE END OF BODY

Starting at tail end of body, with 3.25mm hook and A, make a magic loop.

Row 1 (RS): 1 ch, 6 dc into loop, turn (6 sts).

Row 2 (WS) (inc): 1 ch, 2 dc in each dc, sl st to first st, turn (12 sts). Pull tightly on short end of yarn to close loop.

Row 3 (inc): (Dc2inc, 1 dc) 6 times, turn (18 sts).

Row 4 (inc): 1 ch, (2 lp sts in next dc, 1 lp st in next 2 dc) 6 times, sl st to first st, turn (24 sts).

Row 5 (inc): (Dc2inc, 3 dc) 6 times, turn (30 sts).

Row 6 (inc): 1 ch, (dc2inc, 4 dc) 6 times, sl st to first st, turn (36 sts).

JOIN EAR PIECES

Place the two ear pieces together, with the inner ear facing up.

Next: 1 ch, inserting the hook under both loops of each stitch of the inner ear first, then the outer ear at the same time to join, dc2inc, 1 dc in next 4 dc, dc3inc, 1 dc in next 4 dc, dc2inc (15 sts). Fasten off, leaving a long tail of yarn.

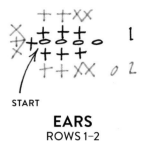

START

EARS
ROWS 1–2

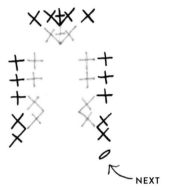

NEXT

JOIN EAR PIECES
INSERT HOOK INTO EACH STITCH
OF BOTH EAR PIECES AT SAME
TIME TO JOIN

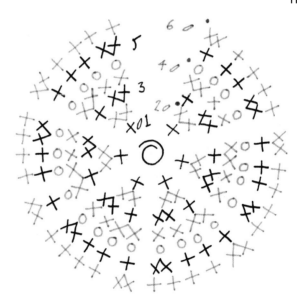

BODY
SHAPE END OF BODY
ROWS 1–6

SHAPE MIDDLE OF BODY

Row 1 (RS): 1 dc in each dc, turn.

Row 2 (WS): 1 ch, 1 lp st in next 12 dc, 1 dc in next 7 dc, 1 lp st in next 10 dc, 1 dc in next 7 dc, sl st to first st, turn.

Row 3: 1 dc in each st, turn.

Row 4: 1 ch, 1 dc in each dc, sl st to first st, turn.

Row 5: Rep row 3.

Rows 6–7: Rep rows 2–3.

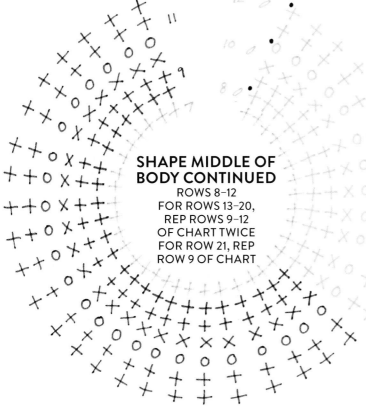

SHAPE MIDDLE OF BODY
ROWS 1–7

SHAPE MIDDLE OF BODY CONTINUED
ROWS 8–12
FOR ROWS 13–20,
REP ROWS 9–12
OF CHART TWICE
FOR ROW 21, REP
ROW 9 OF CHART

Row 8: 1 ch, 1 dc in next 12 dc. Join B in last dc and carry unused yarn on WS of work. 1 dc in next 24 dc with B, sl st to first st, turn.

Row 9: 1 dc in next 24 sts with B, 1 dc in next 12 sts with A, turn.

Row 10: 1 ch, 1 lp st in next 12 dc with A, 1 lp st in next 24 dc with B, sl st to first st, turn.

Row 11: Rep row 9.

Row 12: 1 ch, 1 dc in next 12 dc with A, 1 dc in next 24 dc with B, sl st to first st, turn.

Rows 13–20: Rep rows 9–12 twice.

Row 21: Rep row 9.

Continue with A.

Row 22: 1 ch, 1 lp st in next 12 dc, 1 dc in next 24 dc, sl st to first st, turn.

Rows 23–24: Rep rows 3–4.

Row 25: Rep row 3.

Row 26: Rep row 22.

SHAPE FRONT OF BODY

Row 1 (RS) (dec): (Dc2tog, 4 dc) 6 times, turn (30 sts).

Row 2 (WS) (dec): 1 ch, (dc2tog, 3 dc) 6 times, sl st to first st, turn (24 sts).

Stuff body before continuing.

Row 3 (dec): (Dc2tog, 2 dc) 6 times, turn (18 sts).

Row 4: 1 ch, 1 lp st in each dc, sl st to first st, turn.

Row 5 (dec): (Dc2tog, 1 dc) 6 times, turn (12 sts).

Row 6: Rep row 4.

Break yarn and thread through last 12 stitches. Pull tightly on end of yarn to close. Fasten off.

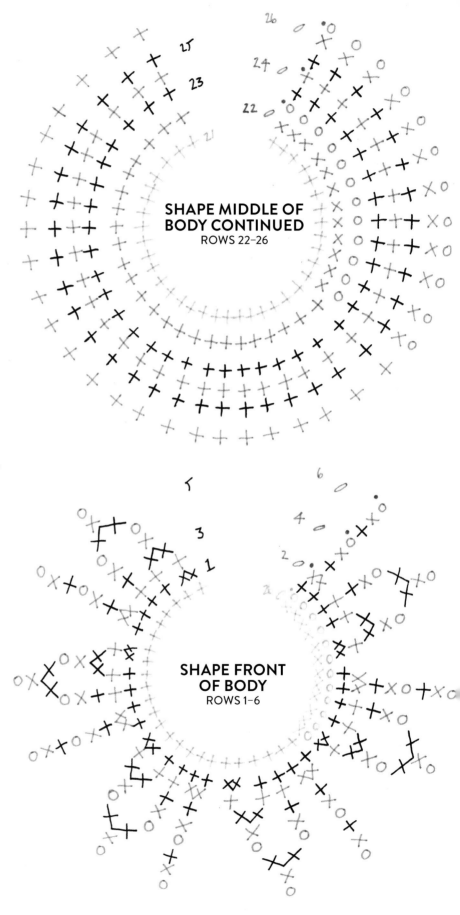

SHAPE MIDDLE OF BODY CONTINUED
ROWS 22–26

SHAPE FRONT OF BODY
ROWS 1–6

Front legs

RIGHT PAW

The bobbles appear on the reverse side of the work. This will be the right side. See page 166 for instructions to make bobble (mb).

Starting at the base of the paw, with 3.25mm hook and A, make a magic loop.

Round 1 (WS): 1 ch, 6 dc into loop (6 sts).

Round 2 (inc): (Dc2inc) 6 times (12 sts). Pull tightly on short end of yarn to close loop.

Round 3 (inc): (Dc2inc, 2 dc) 4 times (16 sts).

Round 4: 1 dc in next 8 dc, (mb, 1 dc in next dc) 4 times, turn.

Round 5 (RS) (dec): 1 ch, 1 dc in first dc, (1 dc in next st, dc2tog) twice, 1 dc in next 9 dc (14 sts).

Round 6 (dec): (1 dc in next dc, dc2tog) twice, 1 dc in next 8 dc (12 sts).

Round 7: 1 dc in each dc.

SHAPE RIGHT LEG

The following is worked in rows.

Row 1 (RS): 1 dc in next 12 dc, turn.

Row 2 (WS): 1 ch, 1 dc in each dc, turn.

Rows 3–5: Rep row 2.

Row 6 (inc): 1 ch, (dc2inc, 3 dc) 3 times, turn (15 sts).

Rows 7–9: 1 ch, 1 dc in each dc, turn.

Row 10: 1 ch, 1 dc in next 4 dc, 1 lp st in next 7 dc, 1 dc in next 4 dc, turn.

Row 11 (inc): 1 ch, (dc2inc, 4 dc) 3 times, turn (18 sts).

Rows 12–13: 1 ch, 1 dc in each dc, turn.

Row 14: 1 ch, 1 dc in next 5 dc, 1 lp st in next 8 dc, 1 dc in next 5 dc, turn.

Rows 15–16: 1 ch, 1 dc in each dc, turn.

Row 17 (dec): 1 ch, (dc2tog, 1 dc) 6 times, turn (12 sts).

Row 18 (dec): 1 ch, (dc2tog) twice, 1 lp st in next 4 dc, (dc2tog) twice (8 sts).

Fasten off, leaving a long tail of yarn at the end.

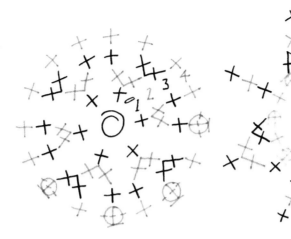

FRONT LEGS
RIGHT PAW
ROUNDS 1–4

FRONT LEGS CONTINUED
RIGHT PAW
ROUNDS 5-7

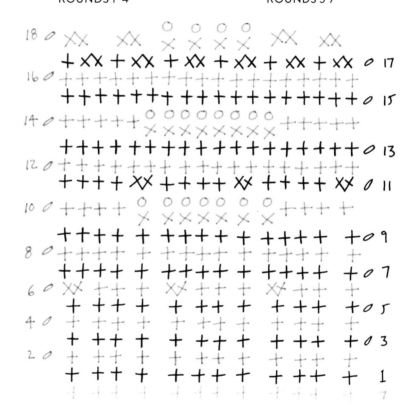

FRONT LEGS CONTINUED
SHAPE RIGHT LEG
ROWS 1–18

LEFT PAW

Starting at the base of the paw, with 3.25mm hook and A, make a magic loop.

Rounds 1–6: Work as for rounds 1–6 of right paw.

Round 7: 1 dc in next 7 dc, finishing 5 sts before the end.

SHAPE LEFT LEG

The following is worked in rows.

Rows 1–18: Work as for rows 1–18 of shape right leg.

Fasten off, leaving a long tail of yarn at the end.

FRONT LEGS CONTINUED
LEFT PAW
ROUND 7

Hind legs

RIGHT LEG

Starting at the base of the paw, with 3.25mm hook and A, make a magic loop.

Rounds 1–7: Work as for rounds 1–7 of right front paw.

Rounds 8–12: 1 dc in each dc.

SHAPE BACK OF LEG

Round 13: 1 dc in next dc, ending at the side of the leg; 6 ch, skip the 6 dc at the front of the leg, 1 dc in next 5 dc.

Round 14: 1 dc in next dc, 1 dc in next 6 ch, 1 dc in next 5 dc.

Break yarn and thread through last round of stitches. Pull tightly on end of yarn to close and fasten off.

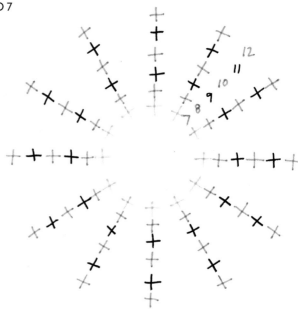

HIND LEGS
RIGHT LEG
ROUNDS 8–12

SHAPE BACK OF LEG
ROUNDS 13–14

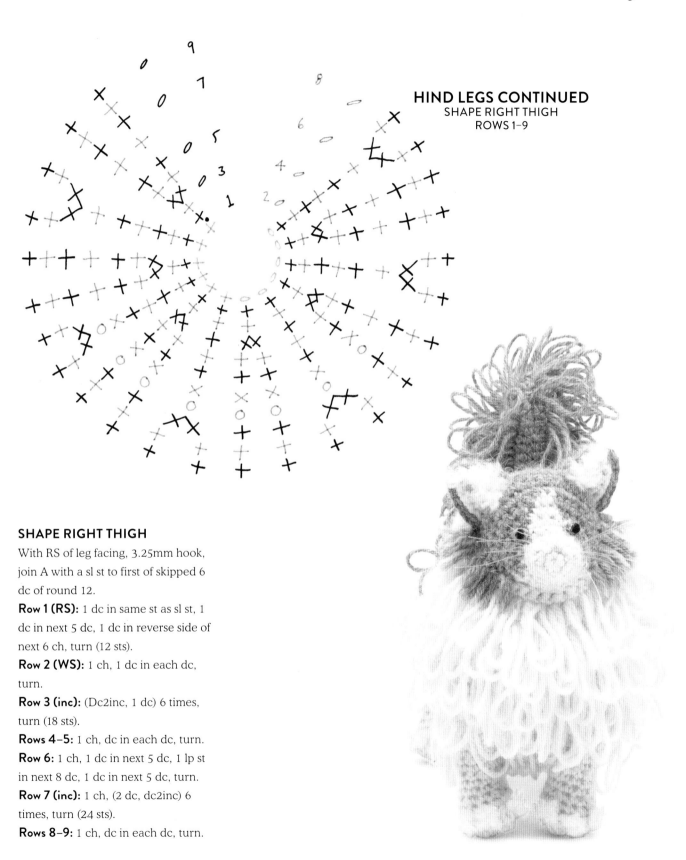

HIND LEGS CONTINUED
SHAPE RIGHT THIGH
ROWS 1–9

SHAPE RIGHT THIGH

With RS of leg facing, 3.25mm hook, join A with a sl st to first of skipped 6 dc of round 12.

Row 1 (RS): 1 dc in same st as sl st, 1 dc in next 5 dc, 1 dc in reverse side of next 6 ch, turn (12 sts).

Row 2 (WS): 1 ch, 1 dc in each dc, turn.

Row 3 (inc): (Dc2inc, 1 dc) 6 times, turn (18 sts).

Rows 4–5: 1 ch, dc in each dc, turn.

Row 6: 1 ch, 1 dc in next 5 dc, 1 lp st in next 8 dc, 1 dc in next 5 dc, turn.

Row 7 (inc): 1 ch, (2 dc, dc2inc) 6 times, turn (24 sts).

Rows 8–9: 1 ch, dc in each dc, turn.

Row 10: 1 ch, 1 dc in next 6 dc, 1 lp st in next 12 dc, 1 dc in next 6 dc, turn.

Row 11 (inc): 1 ch, (dc2inc, 3 dc) 6 times, turn (30 sts).

Rows 12–13: 1 ch, dc in each dc, turn.

Row 14: 1 ch, 1 dc in next 8 dc, 1 lp st in next 14 dc, 1 dc in next 8 dc, turn.

Row 15 (dec): 1 ch, (3 dc, dc2tog) 6 times, turn (24 sts).

Row 16 (dec): 1 ch, (2 dc, dc2tog) 6 times, turn (18 sts).

Row 17 (dec): 1 ch, (1 dc, dc2tog) 6 times, turn (12 sts).

Row 18 (dec): 1 ch, (dc2tog) twice, 1 lp st in next 4 dc, (dc2tog) twice (8 sts).

Fasten off, leaving a long tail of yarn at the end.

LEFT HIND LEG

Starting at the base of the paw, with 3.25mm hook and A, make a magic loop.

Rounds 1–14: Work as for rounds 1–14 of right hind leg.

Break yarn and thread through last round of stitches. Pull tightly on end of yarn to close and fasten off.

SHAPE LEFT THIGH

With RS of leg facing, 3.25mm hook, join A with a sl st to reverse side of first of 6 ch of round 13.

Row 1 (RS): 1 dc in same st as sl st, 1 dc in reverse side of next 5 ch, 1 dc in next 6 skipped dc of round 12, turn (12 sts).

Rows 2–18: Work as for rows 2–18 of right thigh.

Fasten off, leaving a long tail of yarn at the end.

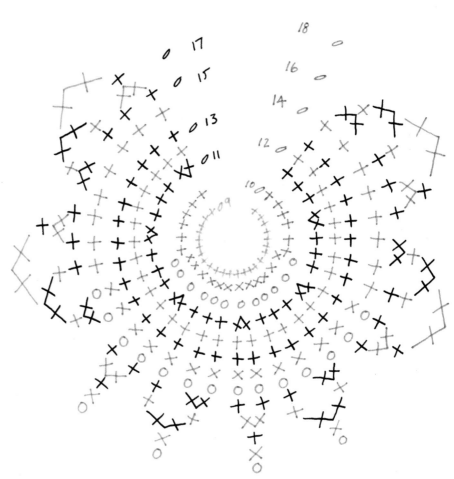

HIND LEGS CONTINUED
SHAPE RIGHT THIGH
ROWS 10–18

HIND LEGS CONTINUED
SHAPE LEFT THIGH
ROW 1

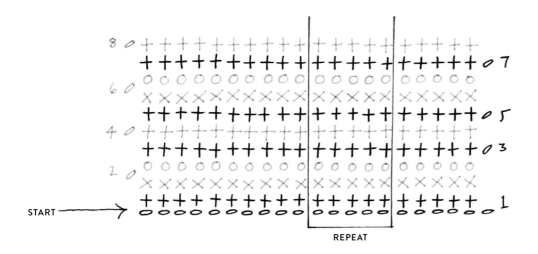

RUFF
ROWS 1–8

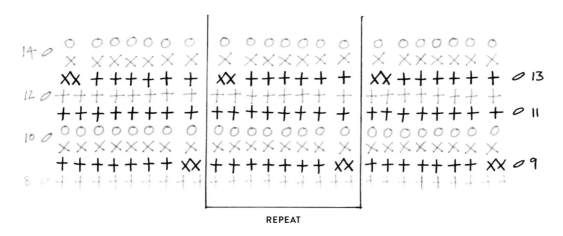

REPEAT

RUFF CONTINUED
ROWS 9–14

Ruff

With 3.25mm hook and A, make
46 ch.
Row 1 (RS): 1 dc in 2nd ch from hook,
1 dc in each ch to end, turn (45 sts).
Row 2 (WS): 1 ch, 1 lp st in each ch
to end, turn.
Rows 3–5: 1 ch, 1 dc in each st, turn.
Rows 6–8: Rep rows 2–4.

Row 9 (dec): 1 ch, (dc2tog, 7 dc) 5
times, turn (40 sts).
Rows 10–12: Rep rows 2–4.
Row 13 (dec): 1 ch, (6 dc, dc2tog) 5
times, turn (35 sts).
Row 14: 1 ch, 1 lp st in each dc.
Fasten off, leaving a long tail each
of yarn.

Tail

With 3.25mm hook and A, make 26 ch.

Row 1 (RS): 1 dc in 2nd ch from hook, 1 dc in next 23 ch, 3 dc in end ch, 1 dc in reverse side of next 24 ch, turn (51 sts).

Row 2 (WS) (inc): 1 ch, 1 lp st in next 25 dc, 3 lp sts in next dc, 1 lp st in next 25 dc, turn (53 sts).

Row 3 (inc): 1 ch, 1 dc in next 26 sts, dc3inc, 1 dc in next 26 sts, turn (55 sts).

Row 4 (inc): 1 ch, 1 lp st in next 27 dc, 3 lp sts in next dc, 1 lp st in next 27 dc, turn (57 sts).

Row 5 (dec): 1 ch, 1 dc in next 26 sts, dc2tog, 1 dc in next st, dc2tog, 1 dc in next 26 sts, turn (55 sts).

Row 6 (dec): 1 ch, 1 lp st in next 26 dc, skip next dc, 1 lp st in next dc, skip next dc, 1 lp st in next 26 dc, turn (53 sts).

Row 7 (dec): 1 ch, 1 dc in next 6 sts, (dc2tog, 1 dc) 5 times, 1 dc in next

3 sts, dc2tog, 1 dc in next st, dc2tog, 1 dc in next 3 sts, (1 dc, dc2tog) 5 times, 1 dc in next 6 sts, turn (41 sts).

Row 8 (dec): 1 ch, 1 lp st in next 19 dc, skip next dc, 1 lp st in next dc, skip next dc, 1 lp st in next 19 dc, turn (39 sts).

Fasten off, leaving a long tail of yarn at the end.

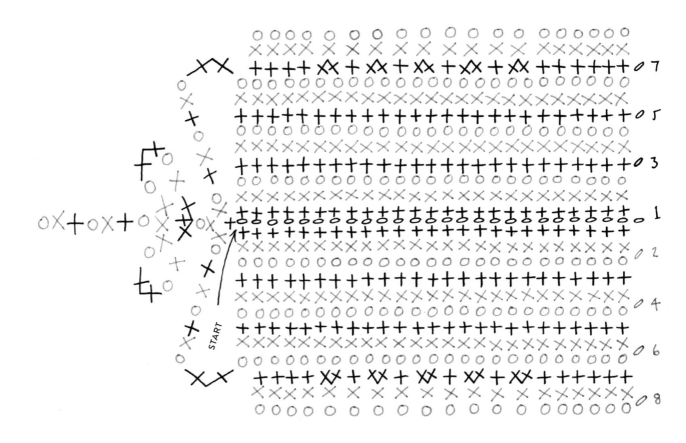

TAIL
ROWS 1–8

Making up

HEAD

Stuff the head. With the tail of yarn left after fastening off, sew the head in place. Stitch all around the neck edges. Tuck the loops that will be covered by the head inside the neck, taking care not to catch the loops that appear around the outside edges of the neck in the stitches. Insert more stuffing into the neck if necessary. Using three strands of embroidery thread, embroider the nose and the pupils of the eyes in satin stitch (see page 170). Work straight stitches around the pupils to form the irises (see page 170).

EARS

Stuff the ears lightly, keeping them flat. Sew the ears in place, near the back of the head, stitching all around the lower edges with the tails of yarn left after fastening off. The fur in the ears is made with tassels (see page 171) that are threaded through the posts of the stitches. Use one 4in (10cm) length of yarn A for each tassel. Attach four tassels to the posts of the stitches of each inner ear. Trim the ends and use a pin to gently separate the fibres.

LEGS

Thread tail of yarn through last row of stitches. Pull tightly on end of yarn to close. Sew the edges of the leg together, matching the rows, stuffing the leg as you sew. Flatten the top of each leg, positioning the seam down the centre of the inside leg, which will be placed against the body. Sew the legs to the body, stitching all around the top of the thighs with the tail of yarn left after fastening off. Take care not to catch any loops in the stitches. The tufts of fluff on the paws are made in the same way as for the ears. Use two 4in (10cm) lengths of A for each tassel. Attach a tassel to the stitch between each toe on the front and back feet. Trim the ends and use a pin to gently separate the fibres.

TAIL

Using the length of yarn left after fastening off, fold the tail lengthways and sew the long edges together with whip stitch (see page 169). Stuff the tail lightly, keeping a flattened shape. Sew the tail in place, stitching all around the edges, taking care not to catch any loops in the stitches and tucking any loops that will be covered inside the tail.

RUFF

With the tail of yarn left after fastening off, sew the short edges of the ruff together, matching the rows. Slip the ruff over the head. Position the last row of the ruff under the chin and align the edge at the back of the ruff with the line of stitches behind the ears. Sew the last row of the ruff to the head, stitching it in place all around the edges. Attach tassels to each side of the face, close to the last row of the ruff, starting in front of the edge of each ear and finishing at the section of the head worked in A. Use one 4in (10cm) length of B for each tassel. Trim the ends of the tassels to neaten, taking care not to cut into the loops of the ruff. These tassels will partly cover the edges of the ruff, softening the line of stitches at the sides of the face.

WHISKERS (OPTIONAL)

Attach three whiskers to the posts of the stitches on each side of the muzzle (see page 171). Trim the ends. Weave in all the yarn ends.

Russian Blue

THE RUSSIAN BLUE HAS LONG SLENDER LEGS AND TAIL, A TRIANGULAR-SHAPED HEAD AND LARGE EARS. THIS CURLED-UP BODY IS CROCHETED IN SHORT ROWS AND, AS THE FEET ARE FACING UP, PAW PADS ARE EMBROIDERED IN SATIN STITCH.

Materials

- Sirdar Snuggly Double Knitting, 55% nylon, 45% acrylic (179yd/165m per 50g ball), or any DK yarn: 1 x 50g ball in 0460 Eeyore (A)
- Metallic stranded embroidery thread in black, such as DMC Light Effects, shade E310, for the nose and eyes
- Stranded embroidery thread in pink-mauve, such as DMC Stranded Cotton, shade 0316, for the paw pads
- 6 lengths of 0.3mm clear nylon thread, each measuring 4¾in (12cm), for the optional whiskers (not suitable for young children)
- 3.25mm (UK10:USD/3) crochet hook
- Blunt-ended yarn needle
- Toy stuffing

Size

- Approximately 5½in (14cm) body length, from top of head to end of body

Tension

22 sts and 24 rows to 4in (10cm) over double crochet using 3.25mm hook. Use a larger or smaller hook if necessary to obtain the correct tension.

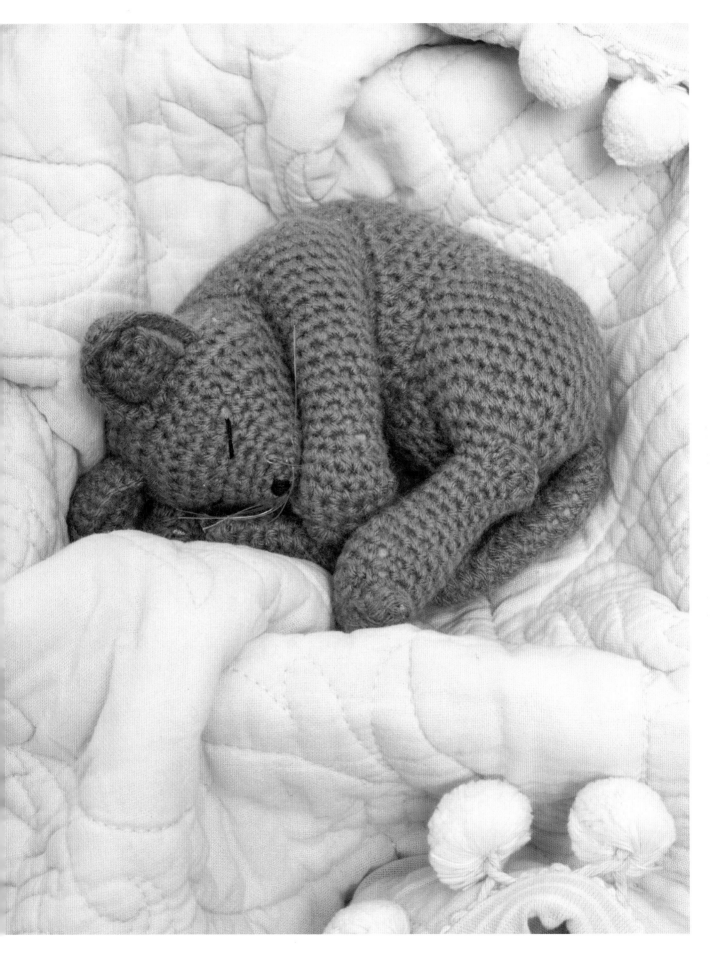

Method

The sleeping Russian Blue's head and body are worked in one piece, in rounds and rows of double crochet. The first row of the body is worked into the stitches at the underside of the muzzle and along the edges of the rows that make up the top of the head. The curled-up body shape is made by crocheting short rows, working into just a few stitches of the previous row and then crocheting into an unworked stitch at the end of each subsequent row. Each ear is made up of two identical crocheted parts that are worked in rows and joined by crocheting into each stitch of both pieces at the same time. Double crochet and half treble stitches form the tapered tail. The curl in the tail is produced by decreasing stitches in the last row. The stitches of the last row of the tail are sewn together and a small amount of stuffing is inserted before sewing it to the body. The toes on the paws are produced by crocheting bobbles that appear on the reverse side of the fabric. The body and tops of the legs should be stuffed lightly so as not to make the sleepy cat too bulky. The eyes, nose and paw pads are embroidered with stranded embroidery threads.

1 ch and 2 ch at beg of the row/round does not count as a st throughout.

Head and body

HEAD

Starting at front of muzzle, with 3.25mm hook and A, make a magic loop (see page 163).

Round 1: 1 ch, 6 dc into loop (6 sts).

Round 2 (inc): (Dc2inc) 6 times (12 sts). Pull tightly on short end of yarn to close loop.

Rounds 3–4: 1 dc in each dc.

Round 5 (inc): (Dc2inc, 3 dc) 3 times (15 sts).

Round 6 (inc): (Dc2inc, 4 dc) 3 times (18 sts).

Round 7: 1 dc in each dc.

Round 8 (inc): (1 dc, dc2inc) 6 times, 1 dc in next 6 dc (24 sts).

Round 9 (inc): (1 dc, dc2inc, 1 dc) 6 times finishing 6 sts before the end, turn (30 sts).

KEY

⌀ CHAIN (CH)

• SLIP STITCH (SL ST)

+ DOUBLE CROCHET (DC)

⤬⤬ DC2INC

⤫⤫ DC2TOG

⊕ MAKE BOBBLE (MB)

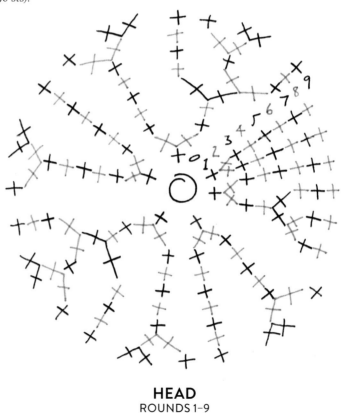

HEAD
ROUNDS 1–9

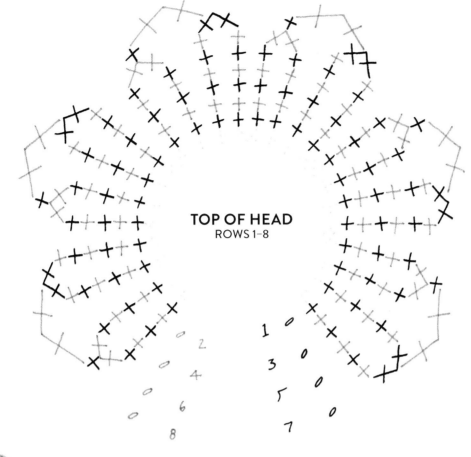

TOP OF HEAD
ROWS 1–8

TOP OF HEAD

Row 1 (WS): 1 ch, 1 dc in next 24 dc, turn.

Continue on these 24 sts.

Row 2 (RS): 1 ch, 1 dc in each dc, turn.

Rows 3–5: Rep last row.

Row 6 (dec): 1 ch, (dc2tog, 2 dc) 6 times, turn (18 sts).

Row 7 (dec): 1 ch, (dc2tog, 1 dc) 6 times, turn (12 sts).

Row 8 (dec): 1 ch, (dc2tog) 6 times (6 sts).

Break yarn and thread through last 6 stitches. Pull tightly on end of yarn. Fasten off.

135

SHAPE TOP OF BODY

With RS of head facing and 3.25mm hook, skip first 3 of unworked 6 dc of round 8 of head and join A with a sl st to next dc.

Row 1 (RS): 2 dc in same st as sl st, 1 dc in next dc, dc2inc, work 14 dc evenly along edge of the rows of head; working in rem 3 unworked sts of round 8 of head, dc2inc, 1 dc in next dc, dc2inc, sl st to first dc, turn (24 sts).

Row 2 (WS): 1 dc in each dc, turn.

Row 3 (inc): 1 ch, (1 dc, dc2inc, 1 dc) twice, 1 dc in next 5 dc, (dc2inc) twice, 1 dc in next 5 dc, (1 dc, dc2inc, 1 dc) twice, sl st to first dc, turn (30 sts).

Row 4: 1 dc in next 17 dc, sl st in next dc, turn.

Row 5: 1 dc in same st as sl st, 1 dc in next 5 dc, sl st in next dc, turn.

Row 6: 1 dc in same st as sl st, 1 dc in next 7 dc, sl st in next dc, turn.

Row 7 (inc): 1 dc in same st as sl st, 1 dc in next 3 dc, (dc2inc) twice, 1 dc in next 4 dc, sl st in next dc, turn (32 sts).

Row 8: 1 dc in same st as sl st, 1 dc in next 13 dc, sl st in next dc, turn.

Row 9: 1 dc in same st as sl st, 1 dc in next 15 dc, sl st in next dc, turn.

Row 10: 1 dc in same st as sl st, 1 dc in next 17 dc, sl st in next dc, turn.

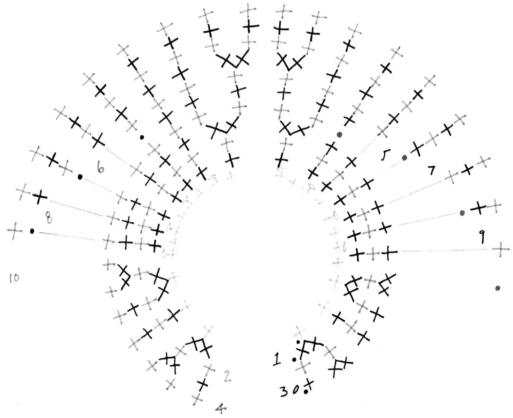

SHAPE TOP OF BODY
ROWS 1–10

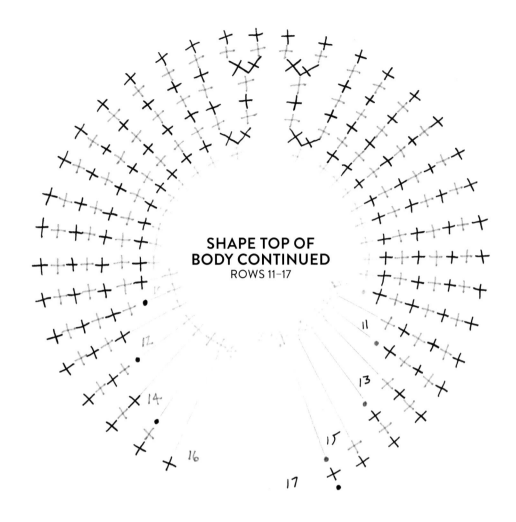

SHAPE TOP OF
BODY CONTINUED
ROWS 11–17

Row 11 (inc): 1 dc in same st as sl st, 1 dc in next 8 dc, (dc2inc) twice, 1 dc in next 9 dc, sl st in next dc, turn (34 sts).

Row 12: 1 dc in same st as sl st, 1 dc in next 23 dc, sl st in next dc, turn.

Row 13: 1 dc in same st as sl st, 1 dc in next 25 dc, sl st in next dc, turn.

Row 14: 1 dc in same st as sl st, 1 dc in next 27 dc, sl st in next dc, turn.

Row 15 (inc): 1 dc in same st as sl st, 1 dc in next 13 dc, (dc2inc) twice, 1 dc in next 14 dc, sl st in next dc, turn (36 sts).

Row 16: 1 dc in same st as sl st, 1 dc in next 33 dc, sl st in next dc, turn.

Row 17: 1 dc in same st as sl st, 1 dc in next 35 dc, sl st to first dc, turn.

SHAPE MIDDLE OF BODY

Row 18: 1 dc in next 22 dc, sl st in next dc, turn.

Row 19: 1 dc in same st as sl st, 1 dc in next 9 dc, sl st in next dc, turn.

Row 20: 1 dc in same st as sl st, 1 dc in next 11 dc, sl st in next dc, turn.

Rows 21–23: Rep rows 8–10.

Row 24: 1 dc in same st as sl st, 1 dc in next 19 dc, sl st in next dc, turn.

Row 25: 1 dc in same st as sl st, 1 dc in next 21 dc, sl st in next dc, turn.

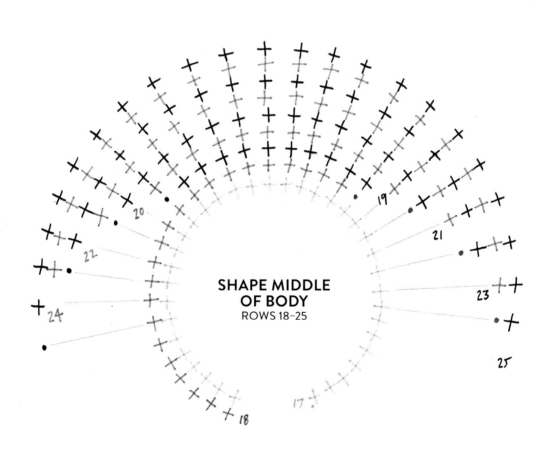

SHAPE MIDDLE OF BODY
ROWS 18–25

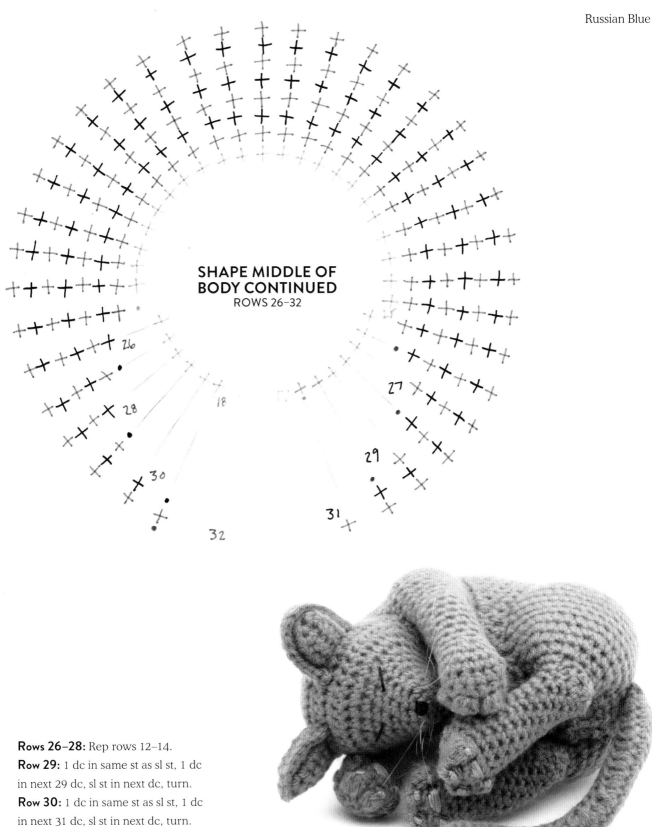

SHAPE MIDDLE OF BODY CONTINUED
ROWS 26–32

Rows 26–28: Rep rows 12–14.

Row 29: 1 dc in same st as sl st, 1 dc in next 29 dc, sl st in next dc, turn.

Row 30: 1 dc in same st as sl st, 1 dc in next 31 dc, sl st in next dc, turn.

Rows 31–32: Rep rows 16–17.

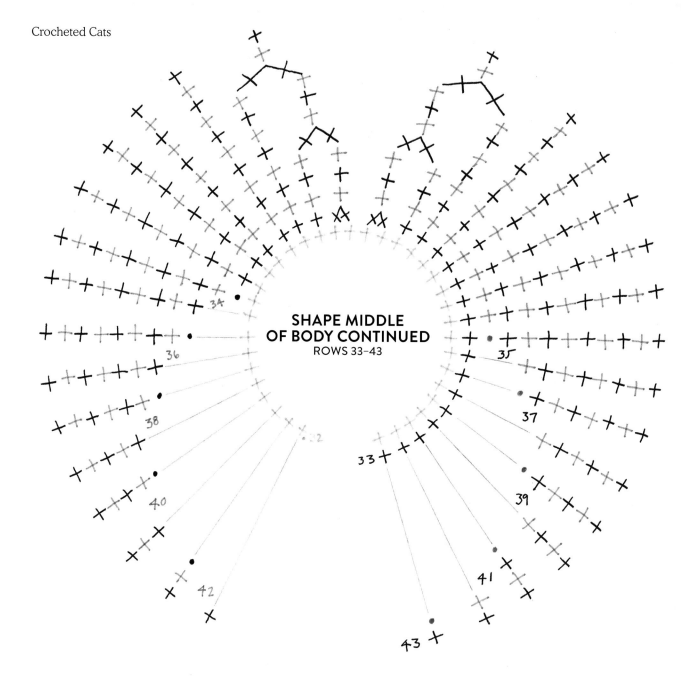

**SHAPE MIDDLE
OF BODY CONTINUED**
ROWS 33–43

Row 33 (dec): 1 dc in next 16 dc,
(dc2tog) twice, 1 dc in next 6 dc, sl st
in next dc, turn (34 sts).

Rows 34–35: Rep rows 9–10.

Row 36: Rep row 24.

Row 37 (dec): 1 dc in same st as sl st,
1 dc in next 8 dc, (dc2tog) twice, 1 dc
in next 9 dc, sl st in next dc, turn
(32 sts).

Row 38: Rep row 25.

Rows 39–40: Rep rows 12–13.

Row 41 (dec): 1 dc in same st as sl st,
1 dc in next 11 dc, (dc2tog) twice, 1
dc in next 12 dc, sl st in next dc, turn
(30 sts).

Row 42: Rep row 14.

Row 43: 1 dc in same st as sl st, 1 dc
in next 29 dc. Do not turn.
Stuff the head and lightly stuff the
body before continuing.

140

SHAPE END OF BODY

The following is worked in rounds.

Round 1 (dec): (Dc2tog, 3 dc) 6 times (24 sts).

Round 2 (dec): (Dc2tog, 2 dc) 6 times (18 sts).

Round 3 (dec): (Dc2tog, 1 dc) 6 times (12 sts).

Round 4 (dec): (Dc2tog) 6 times (6 sts).

Break yarn and thread through last 6 stitches.

Pull tightly on end of yarn to close.

Fasten off.

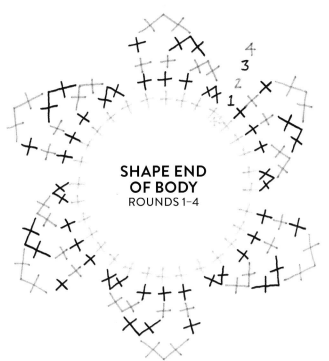

**SHAPE END
OF BODY**
ROUNDS 1–4

Ears (make 2)

With 3.25mm hook and A, make 6 ch.

Row 1: 1 dc in 2nd ch from hook, 1 dc in next 3 ch, 3 dc in next ch, 1 dc in reverse side of next 4 ch, turn (11 sts).

Row 2 (inc): 1 ch, dc2inc, 1 dc in next 4 dc, dc3inc, 1 dc in next 4 dc, dc2inc (15 sts).

Fasten off. This completes the inner ear.

Make one more piece to match the first for the outer ear. Turn work at the end and do not fasten off.

JOIN EAR PIECES

Place the two ear pieces together, with the inner ear facing up.

Next: 1 ch, inserting the hook under both loops of each stitch of the inner ear first, then the outer ear at the same time to join, dc2inc, 1 dc in next 6 dc, dc3inc, 1 dc in next 6 dc, dc2inc (19 sts). Fasten off, leaving a long tail of yarn.

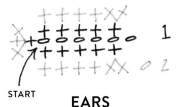

START

EARS
ROWS 1–2

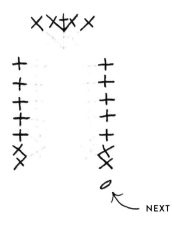

NEXT

JOIN EAR PIECES
INSERT HOOK INTO EACH
STITCH OF BOTH EAR PIECES
AT SAME TIME TO JOIN

Front legs (make 2)

The bobbles appear on the reverse side of the work. This will be the right side. See page 166 for instructions to make bobble (mb).

Starting at the base of the paw, with 3.25mm hook and A, make 6 ch.

Round 1 (WS): 1 dc in 2nd ch from hook, (mb, 1 dc in next ch) twice, 1 dc in reverse side of each ch to end (10 sts).

Round 2 (inc): 1 dc in next dc, mb in same st as last dc, 1 dc in next 3 dc, mb, 1 dc in same st as last st, dc2inc, 1 dc in next 3 dc, dc2inc, turn (14 sts).

Round 3 (RS): 1 ch, 1 dc in each st.

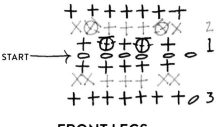

START

FRONT LEGS
ROUNDS 1–3

Round 4: 1 dc in each dc.

Round 5 (dec): (1 dc, dc2tog) twice, 1 dc in next 8 dc (12 sts).

Round 6 (dec): (Dc2tog, 1 dc) twice, 1 dc in next 6 dc (10 sts).

Rounds 7–15: 1 dc in each dc.

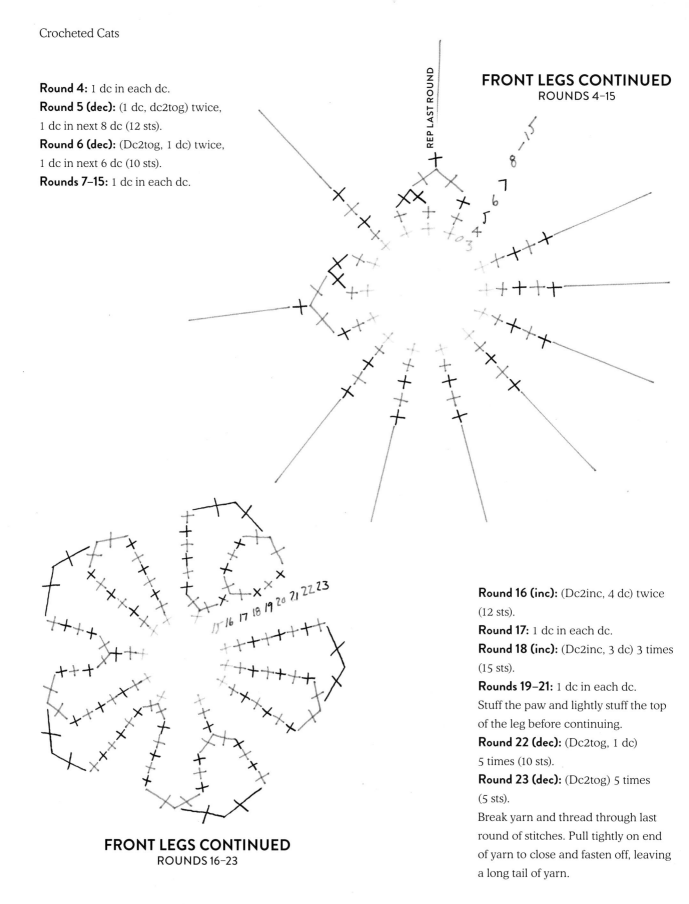

FRONT LEGS CONTINUED
ROUNDS 4–15

FRONT LEGS CONTINUED
ROUNDS 16–23

Round 16 (inc): (Dc2inc, 4 dc) twice (12 sts).

Round 17: 1 dc in each dc.

Round 18 (inc): (Dc2inc, 3 dc) 3 times (15 sts).

Rounds 19–21: 1 dc in each dc. Stuff the paw and lightly stuff the top of the leg before continuing.

Round 22 (dec): (Dc2tog, 1 dc) 5 times (10 sts).

Round 23 (dec): (Dc2tog) 5 times (5 sts).

Break yarn and thread through last round of stitches. Pull tightly on end of yarn to close and fasten off, leaving a long tail of yarn.

HIND LEGS
ROUNDS 5–14

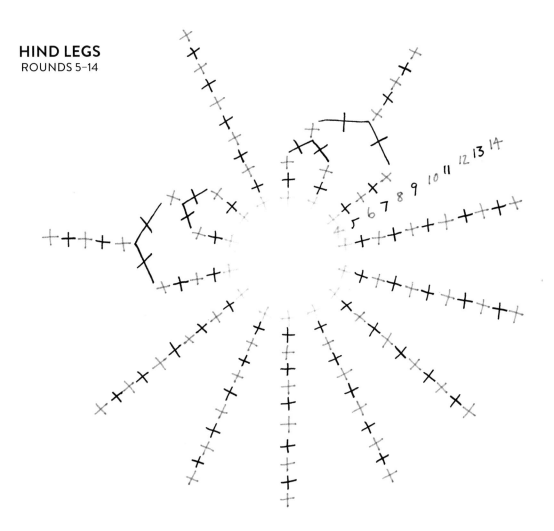

Hind legs

PAW

Starting at the front of the paw, with 3.25mm hook and A, make 6 ch.

Rounds 1–4: Work as for round 1–4 of front legs.

Rounds 5–6: 1 dc in each dc.

Round 7 (dec): (1 dc, dc2tog) twice, 1 dc in next 8 dc (12 sts).

Round 8: 1 dc in each dc.

Round 9 (dec): (Dc2tog, 1 dc) twice, 1 dc in next 6 dc (10 sts).

Rounds 10–14: 1 dc in each dc.

SHAPE BACK OF LEG

Round 15: 1 dc in next 2 dc, ending at the side of the leg; 5 ch, skip the 5 dc at the front of the leg, 1 dc in next 3 dc.

Round 16: 1 dc in next 2 dc, 1 dc in next 5 ch, 1 dc in next 3 dc. Break yarn and thread through last round of stitches. Pull tightly on end of yarn to close and fasten off.

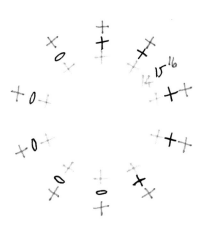

HIND LEGS CONTINUED
SHAPE BACK OF LEG
ROUNDS 15–16

143

SHAPE THIGH

With RS of leg facing, 3.25mm hook, join A with a sl st to first of 5 skipped dc.

Round 1: 1 dc in same st as sl st, 1 dc in next 4 dc, 1 dc in reverse side of next 5 ch (10 sts).

Round 2 (inc): (Dc2inc, 1 dc) 5 times (15 sts).

Round 3 (inc): (Dc2inc, 2 dc) 5 times (20 sts).

Round 4 (inc): (Dc2inc, 3 dc) 5 times (25 sts).

Round 5 (inc): (Dc2inc, 4 dc) 5 times (30 sts).

Rounds 6–11: 1 dc in each dc.

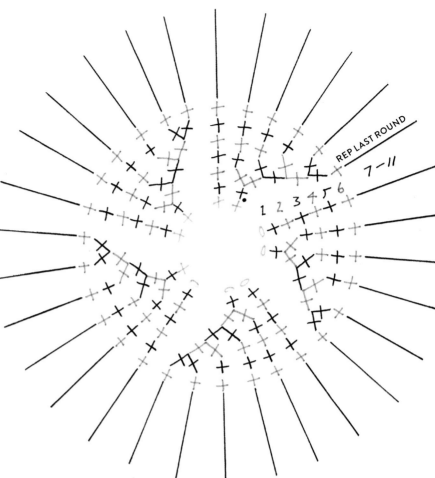

HIND LEGS CONTINUED
SHAPE THIGH
ROUNDS 1–11

Round 12 (dec): (Dc2tog, 3 dc) 6 times (24 sts).

Stuff the paw and lightly stuff the thigh before continuing.

Round 13 (dec): (Dc2tog, 2 dc) 6 times (18 sts).

Round 14 (dec): (Dc2tog, 1 dc) 6 times (12 sts).

Round 15 (dec): (Dc2tog) 6 times (6 sts).

Break yarn and thread through last round of stitches. Pull tightly on end of yarn to close and fasten off, leaving a long tail of yarn.

HIND LEGS CONTINUED
SHAPE THIGH
ROUNDS 12–15

Tail

With 3.25mm hook and A, make 33 ch.

Row 1: 1 dc in 2nd ch from hook, 1 dc in next 30 ch, 3 dc in end ch, 1 dc in reverse side of next 31 ch, turn (65 sts).

Row 2 (dec): 2 ch, 1 htr in next 12 dc, (htr2tog, 1 htr) twice, (dc2tog, 1 dc) twice, 1 dc in next 8 dc, dc3inc, 1 dc in next 8 dc, (1 dc, dc2tog) twice, (1 htr, htr2tog) twice, 1 htr in next 12 dc (59 sts).

Fasten off, leaving a long tail of yarn at the end.

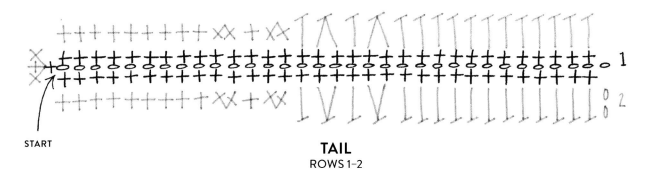

START

TAIL
ROWS 1–2

Making up

HEAD

Embroider the nose in satin stitch (see page 170) using three strands of metallic embroidery thread. With two strands of metallic thread, embroider two straight stitches for each eye (see page 170).

EARS

Stuff the ears lightly, keeping them flat. Sew the ears in place, near the back of the head, stitching all around the lower edges with the tails of yarn left after fastening off.

LEGS

Embroider the paw pads in satin stitch using three strands of embroidery thread. Flatten the top of the legs and sew in place, stitching all around the top of the thighs with the tail of yarn left after fastening off.

TAIL

Using the length of yarn left after fastening off, fold the tail lengthways and sew the long edges together with whip stitch (see page 169). Use the end of the crochet hook to push a small amount of stuffing into the tail. Flatten the top of the tail and sew the edges together. Sew the tail to the end of the body.

WHISKERS (OPTIONAL)

Attach three whiskers to the posts of the stitches on each side of the muzzle (see page 171). Trim the ends. Weave in all the yarn ends.

American Bobtail

THE STRIPED DESIGN ON THE CAT'S BODY IS BASED ON THE CLASSIC TABBY COAT. LOOP STITCH IS USED TO MAKE THE FLUFFY TAIL.

Materials

- Rowan Alpaca Classic, 57% alpaca, 43% cotton (131yd/120m per 25g ball), or any DK yarn:
  1 x 25g ball in 00127 Champagne (A)
  1 x 25g ball in 00118 Cinnamon (B)
- Stranded embroidery thread in golden brown, such as Anchor Stranded Cotton, shade 0890, for the eyes
- Stranded embroidery thread in black, such as Anchor Stranded Cotton, shade 0403, for the pupils
- Stranded embroidery thread in pink, such as Anchor Stranded Cotton, shade 0882, for the nose
- 6 lengths of 0.3mm clear nylon thread, each measuring 4¾in (12cm), for the optional whiskers (not suitable for young children)
- 3.25mm (UK10:USD/3) crochet hook
- Blunt-ended yarn needle
- Toy stuffing
- Stitch marker

Size

- Approximately 7⅞in (20cm) body length, from tip of nose to back of hind legs
- Approximately 6¼in (16cm) tall from top of head (excluding ears)

Tension

23 sts and 23 rows to 4in (10cm) over double crochet using 3.25mm hook. Use a larger or smaller hook if necessary to obtain the correct tension.

Method

The cat's head, body and legs are worked in rounds and rows of double crochet, using two colours to make the tabby pattern. The neck is worked in rows, using two colours, starting by crocheting into the stitches at the underside of the muzzle, and then along the edges of the rows that make up the top of the head. The ears are worked in rows. Each ear is made up of two crocheted parts that are joined by crocheting into each stitch of both pieces at the same time. The tail is crocheted in alternate rounds of double crochet and loop stitch. The loops appear on the reverse side of the tail. The tail is turned right side out and the loops are cut and brushed to make them fluffy. Lengths of yarn are threaded through the ears to form the tufty fur. The legs are worked in continuous rounds of double crochet and the toes on the paws are produced by crocheting bobbles, which appear on the reverse side of the fabric. The work is turned after crocheting the toes and continued on the right side. The eyes and nose are embroidered with embroidery threads.

1 ch and 2 ch at beg of the row/round does not count as a st throughout.

Head

Starting at front of muzzle, with 3.25mm hook and A, make a magic loop (see page 163).
Round 1: 1 ch, 6 dc into loop (6 sts).
Round 2 (inc): (Dc2inc) 6 times (12 sts). Pull tightly on short end of yarn to close loop.
Rounds 3–4: 1 dc in each dc.

SHAPE FACE

The following is worked in rows.
Row 1 (RS): Dc2inc, join B in last dc and carry unused yarn on WS of work, with B work 1 dc in next dc, dc2inc; 1 dc in next 2 dc with A; with B, dc2inc, 1 dc in next dc; with A, dc2inc, 1 dc in next dc, (dc2inc) twice, 1 dc in next dc, turn (18 sts).
Row 2 (WS) (inc): With A, 1 ch, 1 dc in next 6 dc, dc2inc, 1 dc in next dc; dc2inc with B, (1 dc, dc2inc, 1 dc) twice with A, dc2inc with B; with A, 1 dc in next dc, dc2inc, sl st to first dc, turn (24 sts).
Row 3 (inc): Dc2inc, 1 dc in next 2 dc with A, 1 dc in next dc with B, 1 dc in next dc with A; with B, dc2inc, 1 dc in next dc; dc2inc with A, 1 dc in next 2 dc with B, dc2inc with A; with B, 1 dc in next dc, dc2inc; 1 dc in next dc with A, 1 dc in next dc with B; with A, 1 dc in next 2 dc, dc2inc, finishing 6 sts before the end, turn (30 sts).

HEAD
ROUNDS 1–4

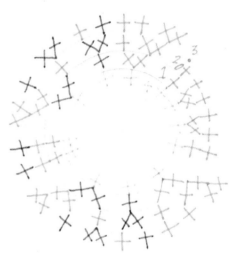

SHAPE FACE
ROWS 1–3

KEY

⟳ MAGIC LOOP

↗ CHAIN (CH)

● SLIP STITCH (SL ST)

+ DOUBLE CROCHET (DC)

⤬ DC2INC

⤬ DC3INC

⤬⤬ DC2TOG

⊕ MAKE BOBBLE (MB)

⧍ LOOP STITCH (LP ST)

COLOUR KEY FOR YARNS

FOR SHAPE FACE, TOP OF HEAD, NECK, SHAPE MIDDLE OF BODY, FRONT LEGS: ROUNDS 8–25, HIND LEGS: SHAPE THIGH

All other charts are shown in alternate rounds/rows of blue and black.

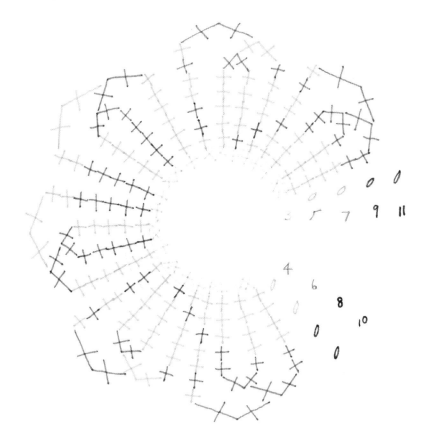

TOP OF HEAD
ROWS 4–11

TOP OF HEAD

Row 4: 1 ch, 1 dc in next 5 dc with A, 1 dc in next dc with B, 1 dc in next 3 dc with A, (1 dc with B, 1 dc with A, 1 dc with B) twice, 1 dc in next 3 dc with A, 1 dc in next dc with B, 1 dc in next 5 dc with A, turn.
Continue on these 24 sts.

Row 5: 1 ch, 1 dc in next 4 dc with A, 1 dc in next dc with B, 1 dc in next 2 dc with A, (1 dc with B, 1 dc with A) twice, 1 dc in next 2 dc with B, (1 dc with A, 1 dc with B) twice, 1 dc in next 2 dc with A, 1 dc in next dc with B, 1 dc in next 4 dc with A, turn.

Row 6: 1 ch, 1 dc in next 3 dc with A, 1 dc in next dc with B, 1 dc in next 3 dc with A, (1 dc with B, 1 dc with A) twice, 1 dc in next 2 dc with B, (1 dc with A, 1 dc with B) twice, 1 dc in next 3 dc with A, 1 dc in next dc with B, 1 dc in next 3 dc with A, turn.

Row 7: 1 ch, 1 dc in next 2 dc with A, 1 dc in next dc with B, 1 dc in next 6 dc with A, (1 dc with B, 1 dc with A, 1 dc with B) twice, 1 dc in next 6 dc with A, 1 dc in next dc with B, 1 dc in next 2 dc with A, turn.

Row 8: 1 ch, 1 dc in next 3 dc with B, 1 dc in next 6 dc with A, (1 dc with B, 1 dc with A, 1 dc with B) twice, 1 dc in next 6 dc with A, 1 dc in next 3 dc with B, turn.

Row 9 (dec): 1 ch, (1 dc, dc2tog, 1 dc) twice with B, 1 dc in next dc with A, dc2tog with B, 1 dc in next 2 dc with A, dc2tog with B, 1 dc in next dc with A, (1 dc, dc2tog, 1 dc) twice with B, turn (18 sts).

Row 10 (dec): 1 ch, *dc2tog with B; with A, 1 dc in next dc, dc2tog, 1 dc in next dc; dc2tog with B*, 1 dc in next 2 dc with A; rep from * to *, turn (12 sts).

Row 11 (dec): 1 ch, (dc2tog) twice with B, (dc2tog) twice with A, (dc2tog) twice with B (6 sts).
Fasten off and thread B through last 6 stitches. Pull tightly on end of yarn and fasten off.

NECK

With RS of head facing, 3.25mm hook and A, sl st to first of unworked 6 dc of row 2 of shape face.

Row 1 (RS): 1 dc in same st as sl st, 1 dc in next 5 dc, work 7 dc evenly along edge of the 8 rows of the first side of the head, joining B in the third st and working last 4 dc with B; work 7 dc evenly along edge of the 8 rows of the other side of the head,

changing to A for the last 3 dc, sl st to first dc, turn (20 sts).

Row 2 (WS): 1 dc in next 3 dc with A, 1 dc in next 8 dc with B, 1 dc in next 9 dc with A, turn.

Row 3 (inc): With A, 1 ch, (1 dc, dc2inc, 1 dc) 3 times; 1 dc in next 8 dc with B; with A work 1 dc in next dc, dc2inc, 1 dc in next dc, sl st to first dc, turn (24 sts).

Row 4: 1 dc in next 4 dc with A, 1 dc in next 8 dc with B, 1 dc in next 12 dc with A, sl st to first dc, turn.

Row 5: 1 dc in next 8 dc with A. Sl st to next st and fasten off, leaving a long tail each of A and B.

Ears

With 3.25mm hook and B, make 4 ch.

Row 1: 1 dc in 2nd ch from hook, 1 dc in next ch, 3 dc in next ch, 1 dc in reverse side of next 2 ch, turn (7 sts).

Row 2 (inc): 1 ch, dc2inc, 1 dc in next 2 dc, dc3inc, 1 dc in next 2 dc, dc2inc (11 sts).

Fasten off, leaving a long tail of yarn. This completes the inner ear.

With A, make one more piece to match the first for the outer ear. Turn work at the end and do not fasten off.

JOIN EAR PIECES

Place the two ear pieces together, with the inner ear facing up.

Next: 1 ch, inserting the hook under both loops of each stitch of the inner ear first, then the outer ear at the same time to join, dc2inc, 1 dc in next 4 dc, dc3inc, 1 dc in next 4 dc, dc2inc (15 sts). Fasten off, leaving a long tail of yarn.

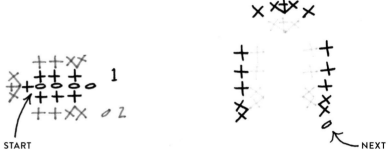

NECK
ROWS 1–5

EARS
ROWS 1–2

JOIN EAR PIECES
INSERT HOOK INTO EACH STITCH OF BOTH EAR PIECES AT SAME TIME TO JOIN

Body

SHAPE FRONT

Starting at front of body, with 3.25mm hook and A, make 10 ch.

Row 1 (RS): 1 dc in 2nd ch from hook, 1 dc in next 7 ch, 2 dc in end ch, 1 dc in reverse side of next 8 ch, turn (18 sts). Place a marker on the tenth stitch to mark the top of the front of the body.

Row 2 (WS) (inc): 1 ch, (dc2inc, 2 dc) 6 times, sl st to first dc, turn (24 sts).

Row 3 (inc): (Dc2inc, 3 dc) 6 times, turn (30 sts).

Row 4 (inc): 1 ch, (dc2inc, 4 dc) 6 times, sl st to first dc, turn (36 sts).

Row 5: 1 dc in each dc, turn.

Row 6: 1 ch, 1 dc in each dc, sl st to first dc, turn.

Rows 7–8: Rep rows 5–6.

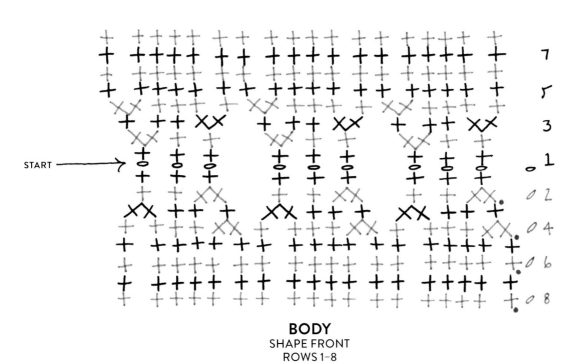

BODY
SHAPE FRONT
ROWS 1–8

SHAPE MIDDLE OF BODY

Row 1 (RS): 1 dc in next 14 dc with A, join B in last dc and work 1 dc in next 3 dc with B, 1 dc in next 2 dc with A, 1 dc in next 3 dc with B, 1 dc in next 14 dc with A, turn.

Row 2 (WS): 1 ch, 1 dc in next 14 dc with A, 1 dc in next 3 dc with B, 1 dc in next 2 dc with A, 1 dc in next 3 dc with B, 1 dc in next 14 dc with A, sl st to first dc, turn.

Row 3: Rep row 1.

Row 4: 1 ch, 1 dc in next 13 dc with A, 1 dc in next 4 dc with B, 1 dc in next 2 dc with A, 1 dc in next 4 dc with B, 1 dc in next 13 dc with A, sl st to first dc, turn.

Row 5: 1 dc in next 7 dc with A, 1 dc in next 10 dc with B, 1 dc in next 2 dc with A, 1 dc in next 10 dc with B, 1 dc in next 7 dc with A, turn.

Row 6: 1 ch, 1 dc in next 6 dc with A, 1 dc in next 11 dc with B, 1 dc in next 2 dc with A, 1 dc in next 11 dc with B, 1 dc in next 6 dc with A, sl st to first dc, turn.

Row 7: 1 dc in next 6 dc with A, 1 dc in next 2 dc with B, 1 dc in next 5 dc with A, 1 dc in next 4 dc with B, 1 dc in next 2 dc with A, 1 dc in next 4 dc with B, 1 dc in next 5 dc with A, 1 dc in next 2 dc with B, 1 dc in next 6 dc with A, turn.

Row 8: 1 ch, 1 dc in next 6 dc with A, 1 dc in next 8 dc with B, 1 dc in next 8 dc with A, 1 dc in next 8 dc with B, 1 dc in next 6 dc with A, sl st to first dc, turn.

Row 9: 1 dc in next 5 dc with A, 1 dc in next 3 dc with B, 1 dc in next 4 dc with A, 1 dc in next 4 dc with B, 1 dc in next dc with A, 1 dc in next 2 dc with B, 1 dc in next dc with A, 1 dc in next 4 dc with B, 1 dc in next 4 dc with A, 1 dc in next 3 dc with B, 1 dc in next 5 dc with A, turn.

Row 10: 1 ch, 1 dc in next 5 dc with A, 1 dc in next 3 dc with B, 1 dc in next 4 dc with A, 1 dc in next 2 dc with B, 1 dc in next dc with A, (1 dc with B, 1 dc with A, 1 dc with B) twice, 1 dc in next dc with A, 1 dc in next 2 dc with B, 1 dc in next 4 dc with A, 1 dc in next 3 dc with B, 1 dc in next 5 dc with A, sl st to first dc, turn.

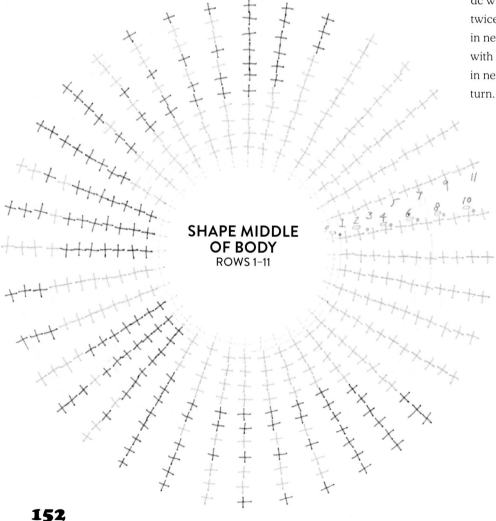

SHAPE MIDDLE
OF BODY
ROWS 1–11

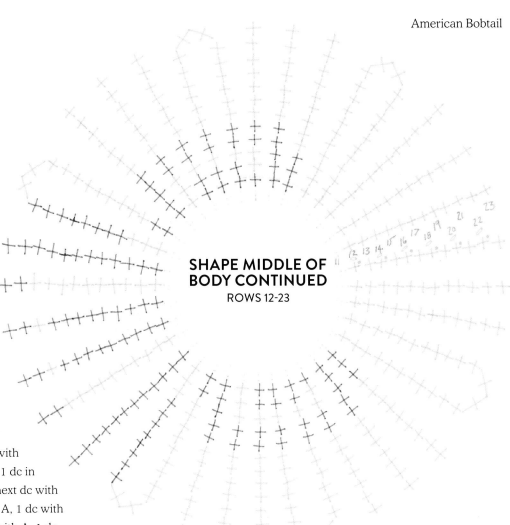

SHAPE MIDDLE OF BODY CONTINUED
ROWS 12-23

Row 11: *1 dc in next 5 dc with A, 1 dc in next 6 dc with B, 1 dc in next dc with A, 1 dc in next 2 dc with B, 1 dc in next dc with A, (1 dc with B, 1 dc with A, 1 dc with B) twice, 1 dc in next dc with A, 1 dc in next 2 dc with B, 1 dc in next dc with A, 1 dc in next 6 dc with B, 1 dc in next 5 dc with A*, turn.

Row 12: 1 ch; rep from * to * of row 11, sl st to first dc, turn.

Row 13: 1 dc in next 5 dc with A, 1 dc in next 2 dc with B, 1 dc in next dc with A, 1 dc in next 3 dc with B, 1 dc in next dc with A, 1 dc in next 2 dc with B, 1 dc in next dc with A, (1 dc with B, 1 dc with A, 1 dc with B) twice, 1 dc in next dc with A, 1 dc in next 2 dc with B, 1 dc in next with A, 1 dc in next 3 dc with B, 1 dc in next dc with A, 1 dc in next 2 dc with B, 1 dc in next 5 dc with A, turn.

Row 14: 1 ch, 1 dc in next 5 dc with A, 1 dc in next 2 dc with B, 1 dc in next 5 dc with A, 1 dc in next dc with B, 1 dc in next 2 dc with A, (1 dc with B, 1 dc with A, 1 dc with B) twice, 1 dc in next 2 dc with A, 1 dc in next dc with B, 1 dc in next 5 dc with A, 1 dc in next 2 dc with B, 1 dc in next 5 dc with A, sl st to first dc, turn.

Row 15: *1 dc in next 6 dc with A, 1 dc in next 7 dc with B, (1 dc with A, 2 dc with B) 3 times, 1 dc in next dc with A, 1 dc in next 7 dc with B, 1 dc in next 6 dc with A*, turn.

Row 16: 1 ch; rep from * to * of row 15, sl st to first dc, turn.

Row 17: *1 dc in next 14 dc with A, (2 dc with B, 1 dc with A) 3 times, 1 dc in next 13 dc with A*, turn.

Row 18: 1 ch; rep from * to * of row 17, sl st to first dc, turn.

Rows 19–20: Rep last 2 rows.

Row 21: 1 dc in next 14 dc with A, 1 dc in next 2 dc with B, 1 dc in next 4 dc with A, 1 dc in next 2 dc with B, 1 dc in next 14 dc with A, turn.

Row 22: 1 ch, 1 dc in next 14 dc with A, 1 dc in next 8 dc with B, 1 dc in next 14 dc with A, sl st to first dc, turn.

Row 23 (dec): (3 dc, dc2tog) 3 times with A, 1 dc in next 6 dc with B, (dc2tog, 3 dc) 3 times with A, do not turn (30 sts).

SHAPE END OF BODY

The following is worked in rounds.

Continue with A.

Round 1 (dec): (Dc2tog, 3 dc) 6 times
(24 sts).

Stuff body before continuing.

Round 2 (dec): (Dc2tog, 2 dc) 6 times
(18 sts).

Round 3 (dec): (Dc2tog, 1 dc) 6 times
(12 sts).

Round 4 (dec): (Dc2tog) 6 times
(6 sts).

Break yarn and thread through last
6 stitches. Pull tightly on end of yarn
to close. Fasten off.

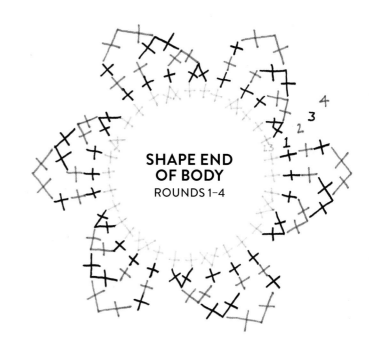

**SHAPE END
OF BODY**
ROUNDS 1–4

Front legs

The bobbles appear on the reverse side
of the work. This will be the right side.
See page 166 for instructions to make
bobble (mb).

Starting at the base of the paw, with
3.25mm hook and A, make a magic loop.

Round 1 (WS): 1 ch, 6 dc into loop (6 sts).

Round 2 (inc): (Dc2inc) 6 times
(12 sts). Pull tightly on short end of
yarn to close loop.

Round 3 (inc): (Dc2inc, 2 dc) 4 times
(16 sts).

Round 4: 1 dc in next 8 dc, (mb, 1 dc in
next dc) 4 times, turn.

Round 5 (RS) (dec): 1 ch, 1 dc in first dc,
(1 dc in next st, dc2tog) twice, 1 dc in next
9 dc (14 sts).

Round 6 (dec): (1 dc in next dc, dc2tog)
twice, 1 dc in next 8 dc (12 sts).

Round 7: 1 dc in each dc. Join B in last dc
and carry unused yarn on WS of work.

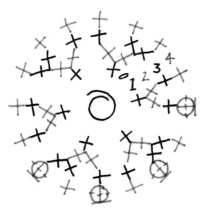

FRONT LEGS
ROUNDS 1–4

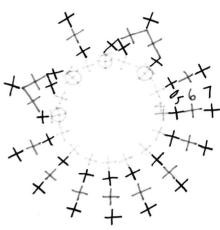

FRONT LEGS CONTINUED
ROUNDS 5–7

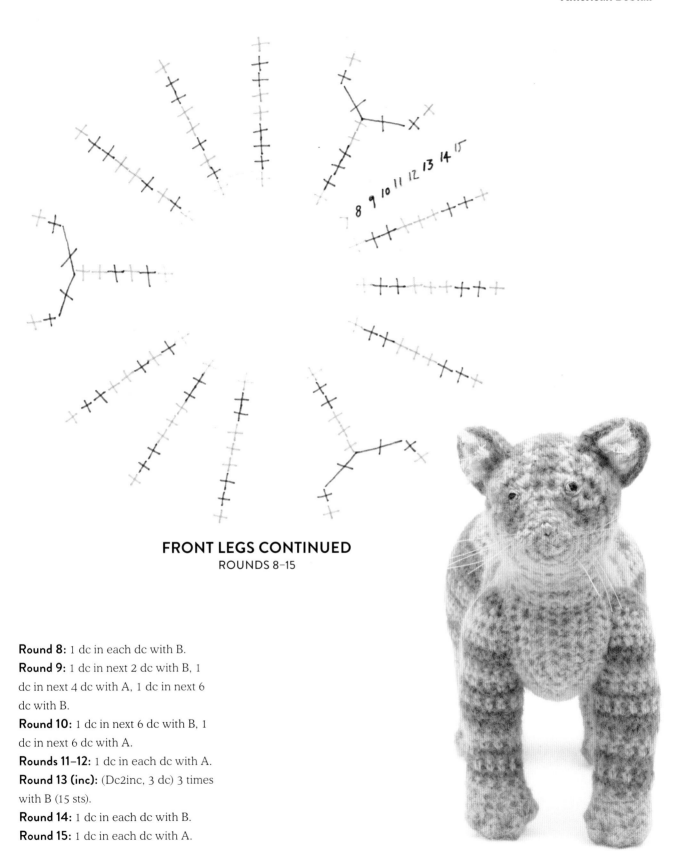

FRONT LEGS CONTINUED
ROUNDS 8–15

Round 8: 1 dc in each dc with B.

Round 9: 1 dc in next 2 dc with B, 1 dc in next 4 dc with A, 1 dc in next 6 dc with B.

Round 10: 1 dc in next 6 dc with B, 1 dc in next 6 dc with A.

Rounds 11–12: 1 dc in each dc with A.

Round 13 (inc): (Dc2inc, 3 dc) 3 times with B (15 sts).

Round 14: 1 dc in each dc with B.

Round 15: 1 dc in each dc with A.

FRONT LEGS CONTINUED
ROUNDS 16-25

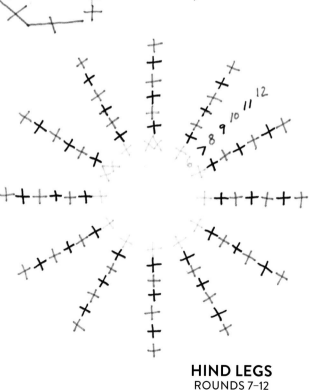

Rounds 16-17: Rep rounds 14-15.

Round 18 (inc): (Dc2inc, 4 dc) 3 times with A (18 sts).

Round 19: 1 dc in next 6 dc with A, 1 dc in next 12 dc with B.

Round 20: 1 dc in each dc with B.

Rounds 21-23: 1 dc in each with A. Stuff leg before continuing. Continue with B.

Round 24 (dec): (Dc2tog, 1 dc) 6 times (12 sts).

Round 25 (dec): (Dc2tog) 6 times (6 sts).

Break yarn and thread through last round of stitches. Pull tightly on end of yarn to close. Fasten off, leaving a long tail of A at the end.

Hind legs (make 2)

Starting at the base of the paw, with 3.25mm hook and A, make a magic loop.

Rounds 1-6: Work as for rounds 1-6 of front legs.

Rounds 7-12: 1 dc in each dc.

HIND LEGS
ROUNDS 7-12

SHAPE BACK OF LEG

Round 13: 1 dc in next dc, ending at the side of the leg; 6 ch, skip the 6 dc at the front of the leg, 1 dc in next 5 dc.

Round 14: 1 dc in next dc, 1 dc in next 6 ch, 1 dc in next 5 dc. Break yarn and thread through last round of stitches. Pull tightly on end of yarn to close and fasten off

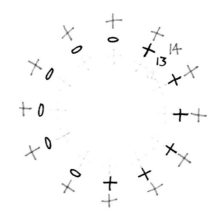

HIND LEGS CONTINUED
SHAPE BACK OF LEG
ROUNDS 13–14

SHAPE THIGH

With RS of leg facing, 3.25mm hook, and A, sl st in first of skipped 6 dc of round 12.

Round 1: 1 dc in same st as sl st, 1 dc in next 5 dc, 1 dc in reverse side of next 6 ch (12 sts).

Round 2: 1 dc in each dc. Join B in last dc.

Round 3 (inc): (Dc2inc, 1 dc) 4 times with B, (dc2inc, 1 dc) twice with A (18 sts).

Round 4: 1 dc in each dc with A.

Round 5: 1 dc in next 2 dc with A, 1 dc in next 8 dc with B, 1 dc in next 8 dc with A.

Round 6 (inc): (Dc2inc, 2 dc) 6 times with B (24 sts).

Rounds 7–8: 1 dc in each dc with A.

Round 9: 1 dc in each dc with B.

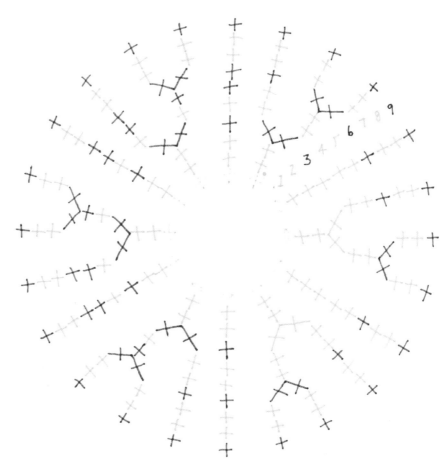

HIND LEGS CONTINUED
SHAPE THIGH
ROUNDS 1–9

Round 10 (inc): (Dc2inc, 3 dc) twice with B, (dc2inc, 3 dc) twice with A, (dc2inc, 3 dc) twice with B (30 sts).

Round 11: 1 dc in next 5 dc with A, 1 dc in next 7 dc with B, 1 dc in next 6 dc with A, 1 dc in next 7 dc with B, 1 dc in next 5 dc with A.

Round 12: 1 dc in next 9 dc with A, 1 dc in next 12 dc with B, 1 dc in next 9 dc with A.

Rounds 13–14: 1 dc in each dc with B.

Round 15 (dec): (Dc2tog, 3 dc) 6 times with A (24 sts).

Stuff leg before continuing.

Round 16 (dec): (Dc2tog, 2 dc) 6 times with A (18 sts).

Continue with B.

Round 17 (dec): (Dc2tog, 1 dc) 6 times (12 sts).

Round 18 (dec): (Dc2tog) 6 times (6 sts).

Break yarn and thread through last round of stitches. Pull tightly on end of yarn to close and fasten off, leaving a long tail of A at the end.

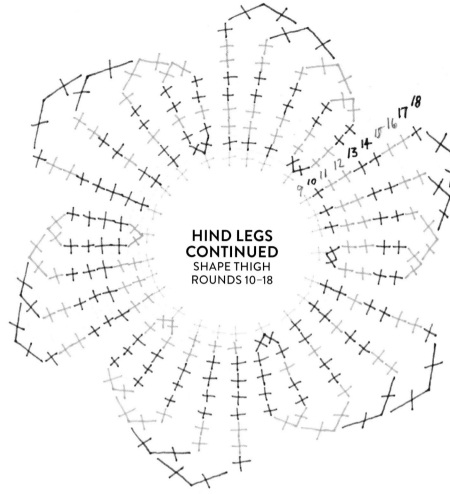

HIND LEGS CONTINUED
SHAPE THIGH
ROUNDS 10–18

Tail

The loops appear on the reverse side of the work. This will be the right side. With 3.25mm hook and A, make a magic loop.

Round 1 (WS): 1 ch, 6 dc into loop (6 sts).

Round 2: 1 lp st in each dc.

Round 3 (inc): (Dc2inc) 6 times (12 sts).

Round 4: 1 lp st in each dc.

Round 5: 1 dc in each st. Join B in last dc.

Continue with B.

Round 6: 1 lp st in each dc.

Round 7: 1 dc in each st.

Rounds 8–9: Rep last 2 rounds.

Round 10: Rep round 6.

Sl st to first st and fasten off, leaving a long tail of B at the end.

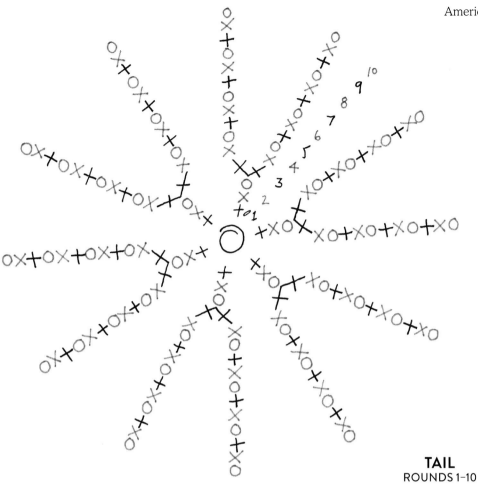

TAIL
ROUNDS 1–10

Making up

HEAD

Stuff the head. With the tails of yarn left after fastening off, sew the head in place on top of the front of the body, indicated by the marker. Stitch all around the neck edges. Insert more stuffing into the neck if necessary. Using three strands of embroidery thread, embroider the nose and the pupils of the eyes in satin stitch (see page 170). Work straight stitches around the pupils to form the irises (see page 170).

EARS

Stuff the ears lightly, keeping them flat. Sew the ears in place, near the back of the head, stitching all around the lower edges with the tails of yarn left after fastening off. The tufts of fur in the ears are made with tassels (see page 171) that are threaded through the posts of the stitches. Use one 4in (10cm) length of yarn A for each tassel. Attach four tassels to the posts of the stitches of each inner ear. Trim the ends and use a pin to gently separate the fibres.

LEGS

Flatten the top of the legs and sew in place, stitching all around the top of the thighs.

TAIL

Turn the work right side out. Cut through the loops and brush the strands of yarn to fluff them. Trim the ends of the brushed yarn. Insert a small amount of stuffing into the tail. Sew the tail in place using the length of yarn left after fastening off.

WHISKERS (OPTIONAL)

Attach three whiskers to the posts of the stitches on each side of the muzzle (see page 171). Trim the ends. Weave in all the yarn ends.

Getting Started

CHECK THE LIST OF MATERIALS AT THE BEGINNING OF EACH PATTERN TO SEE WHAT YOU WILL NEED TO MAKE YOUR CROCHETED CAT. HERE IS SOME INFORMATION TO HELP YOU GET STARTED WITH THE PROJECTS.

Hooks

Crochet hook sizes vary widely, from tiny hooks that produce a very fine stitch when used with threads, to oversized hooks for working with several strands of yarn at a time to create a bulky fabric. Using a larger or smaller hook will change the look of the fabric; it will also affect the tension and the amount of yarn re-quired. The projects in this book use just one size: 3.25mm (UK10:USD/3).

Needles

A blunt-ended yarn needle is used to sew the projects together. The large eye makes it easy to thread the needle and the rounded end will prevent any snagging.

Substituting yarns

When substituting yarns, it is important to calculate the number of balls required by the number of yards or metres per ball, rather than the weight of the yarn, because this varies according to the fibre. Tension is also important. Always work a tension swatch (see opposite) in the yarn you wish to use before starting a project.

Reading charts

Each symbol on a chart represents a stitch; each round or row represents one round or row of crochet.

For rounds of crochet, read the chart anti-clockwise, starting at the centre and working out to the last round on the chart.

For rows of crochet, the chart should be read back and forth, following the number at the beginning of each row.

The charts are shown in alternate rounds or rows of blue and black. The last round or row from a previous chart is shown in grey. Where multiple colour changes are used, the stitches on the charts are shown in the colour to represent each yarn.

Tension

It is vital to check your tension before starting a project, as this will affect the size and look of the cat, as well as the amount of yarn you will use. The tension is the number of rows and stitches per square inch or centimetre of crocheted fabric. Using the same size hook and type of stitch as in the pattern, work a sample of around 5in (12.5cm) square and then smooth out on a flat surface.

STITCHES

Place a ruler horizontally across the work and mark 4in (10cm) with pins. Count the number of stitches between the pins, including half stitches. This will give you the tension of stitches.

ROWS

Measure the tension of rows by placing a ruler vertically over the work and mark 4in (10cm) with pins. Count the number of rows between the pins.

If the number of stitches and rows is greater than those stated in the pattern, your tension is tighter and you should use a larger hook. If the number of stitches and rows is fewer than those stated in the pattern, your tension is looser, so you should use a smaller hook.

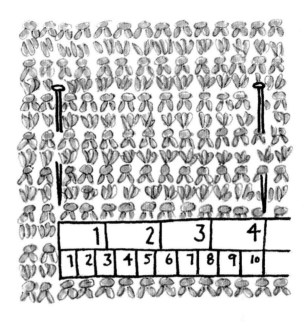

STITCHES

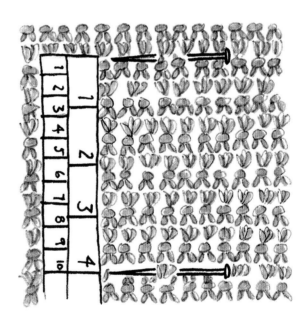

ROWS

161

Crochet Stitches

HERE YOU WILL FIND MORE DETAILS ON THE TECHNIQUES USED TO CROCHET THE CATS, INCLUDING HOW TO HOLD THE HOOK AND YARN, AND CROCHETING THE VARIOUS STITCHES.

Slip knot

Take the end of the yarn and form it into a loop. Holding it in place between thumb and forefinger, insert the hook through the loop, catch the long end that is attached to the ball, and draw it back through. Keeping the yarn looped on the hook, pull through until the loop closes around the hook, ensuring it is not tight. Pulling on the short end of yarn will loosen the knot, while pulling on the long end will tighten it.

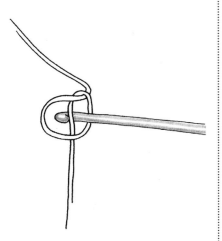

Holding the hook

Hold the hook as you would a pencil, bringing your middle finger forward to rest near the tip of the hook. This will help control the movement of the hook, while the fingers of your other hand will regulate the tension of the yarn. The hook should face you, pointing slightly downwards. The motion of the hook and yarn should be free and even, not tight. This will come with practice.

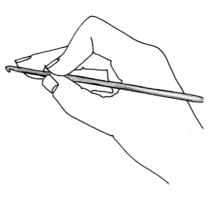

Holding the yarn

To hold your work and control the tension, pass the yarn over the first two fingers of your left hand (right if you are left-handed), under the third finger and around the little finger, and let the yarn fall loosely to the ball. As you work, take the stitch you made between the thumb and forefinger of the same hand.

The hook is usually inserted through the top two loops of a stitch as you work, unless otherwise stated in a pattern. A different effect is produced when only the back or front loop of the stitch is picked up.

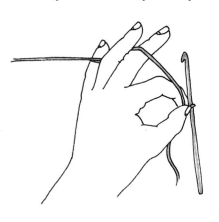

Magic loop

Many of the crocheted pieces start with an adjustable loop of yarn. To make the loop, wind the yarn around a finger, insert the hook, catch the yarn and draw back through the loop. After a couple of rounds have been crocheted, covering the loop of yarn, the short end of yarn is pulled tight to close the centre. An alternative method is to make four chain stitches and then slip stitch to the first chain to form a ring. However, this technique does leave a hole in the middle.

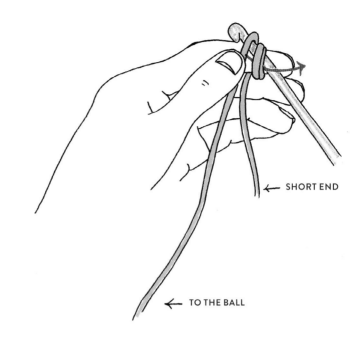

← SHORT END

← TO THE BALL

Chain (ch)

1 Pass the hook under and over the yarn that is held taut between the first and second fingers. This is called yarn round hook (yrh). Draw the yarn through the loop on the hook. This makes one chain (ch).

2 Repeat step 1, keeping the thumb and forefinger of the left hand close to the hook, until you have as many chain stitches as required.

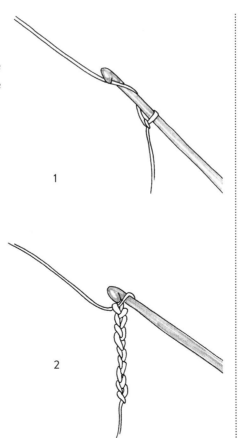

1

2

Slip stitch (sl st)

Make a practice chain of 10. Insert hook into first stitch (st), yrh, draw through both loops on hook. This forms one slip stitch (sl st). Continue to end. This will give you 10 slip stitches (10 sts).

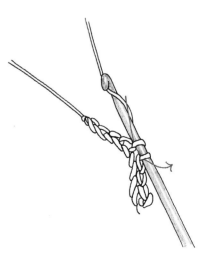

Double crochet (dc)

Make a practice chain of 17. Skip the first ch.

1 Insert hook from front into the next stitch, yrh and draw back through the stitch (two loops on hook).

2 Yrh and draw through two loops (one loop on hook). This makes one double crochet (dc).

Repeat steps 1 and 2 to the end of the row. On the foundation chain of 17 sts, you should have 16 double crochet sts (16 sts).

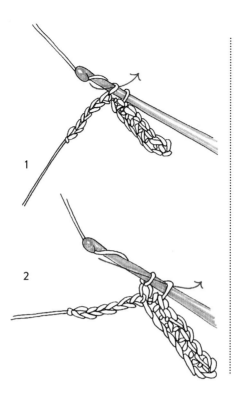

NEXT ROW

Turn the work so the reverse side faces you. Make 1 ch. This is the turning chain; it helps keep a neat edge and does not count as a stitch. Rep steps 1 and 2 to the end of the row. Continue until the desired number of rows is complete. Fasten off.

Fastening off

When you have finished, fasten off by cutting the yarn around 4¾in (12cm) from the work. Draw the loose end through the remaining loop, pulling it tightly.

Half treble (htr)

Make a practice chain of 17. Skip the first 2 ch (these count as the first half treble stitch).

1 Yrh, insert hook into the next stitch, yrh and draw back through stitch (three loops on hook).

2 Yrh, draw through all three loops (one loop on hook). This forms 1 half treble (htr).

Repeat steps 1 and 2 to the end of the row.

On the foundation chain of 17 sts, you should have 16 half trebles

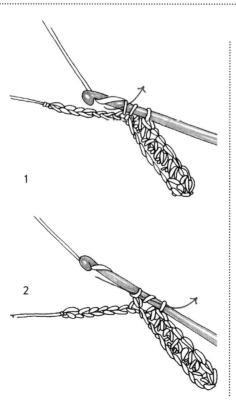

(16 sts), including the 2 ch at the beginning of the row, which is counted as the first stitch.

NEXT ROW

Turn the work so the reverse side faces you. Make 2 ch to count as the first half treble. Skip the first stitch of the previous row. Repeat steps 1 and 2 for the next 14 htr of the last row, work 1 htr in the second of the 2 ch at the end of the row. Continue until the desired number of rows is complete. Fasten off.

Treble (tr)

Make a practice chain of 18. Skip the first 3 ch stitches (these count as the first tr).

1 Yrh, insert hook into the next stitch, yrh and draw back through the stitch (three loops on hook).

2 Yrh, draw through two loops (two loops on hook).

3 Yrh, draw through two loops (one loop on hook). This forms 1 treble (tr).

Repeat steps 1–3 to end of row. On the foundation chain of 18 sts you should have 16 trebles (16 sts), including the 3 ch at the beginning of the row, which is counted as the first stitch.

NEXT ROW
Turn the work so the reverse side faces you. Make 3 ch to count as the first treble. Skip the first stitch of the previous row. Repeat steps 1–3 to the end of the row, working 1 tr into the third of the 3 ch at the beginning of the last row. Continue until the desired number of rows is complete. Fasten off.

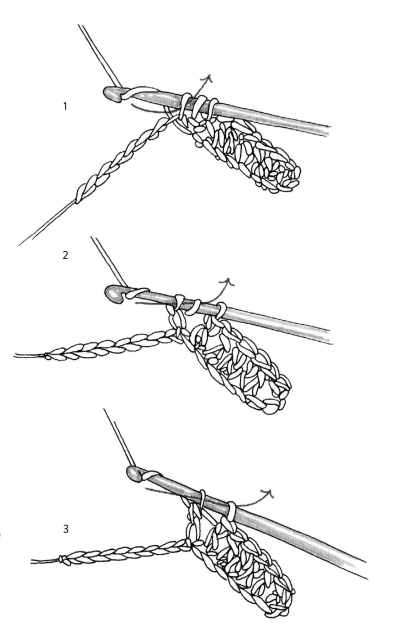

Bobbles

The bobbles appear on the reverse side of the work. This will be the right side.

MAKE BOBBLE (MB)

This stitch is used to create the toes on the paws of all but one of the cats. The bobble is formed by working three treble stitches together in one stitch.

Follow steps 1–2 of treble stitch.

Yrh, insert hook into same st, yrh and draw back through stitch (four loops on hook), yrh and draw through two loops (three loops on hook); rep from * to * (four loops on hook) yrh, draw through all four loops (one loop on hook). This forms one bobble.

MAKE LARGE BOBBLE (MLB)

This stitch is used to create the toes on the Maine Coon's paws (page 55). The bobbles are made in the same way as for the other cats, with four treble stitches worked together in the same stitch.

Follow steps 1–2 of treble stitch

Rep from * to * of row 3 of make bobble three times (five loops on hook) yrh, draw through all five loops (one loop on hook). This forms one large bobble.

Loop stitch (lp st)

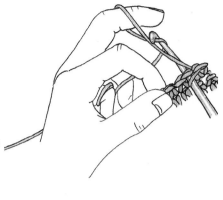

The loops appear on the reverse side of the work. This will be the right side. This method is used to create the long, soft coat of the Ragdoll cat (see pages 122–4). The same stitch is used on the American Bobtail's fluffy tail (see pages 158–9). The loops are cut, producing single strands of yarn.

Insert hook into next dc, with yarn wrapped around finger of yarn hand (see Holding the yarn, page 162), from front to back. Catch the strand at the back of the finger and the strand at the front at the same time, and draw both strands of yarn through the stitch (three loops on hook). Slip loop off finger, yrh and draw through all three loops on hook.

Increasing

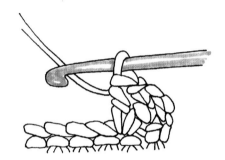

To increase one double crochet (dc2inc), work two stitches into one stitch of the previous row. To increase two double crochet stitches (dc3inc), work three stitches into one stitch of the previous row.

Decreasing

DECREASE ONE DOUBLE CROCHET (DC2TOG)

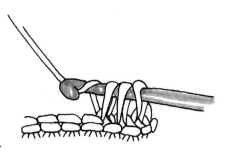

Insert the hook into the next st, yrh and draw back through the stitch (two loops on hook).

Insert the hook into the following st, yrh and draw back through the st (three loops on hook).

Yrh and draw through all three loops.

DECREASE FIVE DOUBLE CROCHET (DC6TOG)

This is used on the sitting cats, pages 66 and 90.

Follow steps 1–2 of dc2tog.

Rep step 2 four more times (seven loops on hook).

Yrh and draw through all seven loops.

DECREASE ONE HALF TREBLE (HTR2TOG)

Yrh, insert the hook into the next st, yrh and draw back through the stitch (three loops on hook); yrh and insert the hook into the following st, yrh and draw back through the stitch (five loops on hook), yrh and draw through all five loops on the hook.

Working into the back or front loop only

The front loop of a stitch is the one closer to you; the back loop is the stitch further away. Generally, the hook is inserted into both loops of a stitch, but when only one loop is crocheted into, the horizontal bar of the remaining loop is left on the surface of the fabric. This method is used on the Maine Coon's muzzle on page 48.

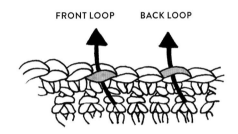

FRONT LOOP   BACK LOOP

Working with multiple colours

JOINING A NEW COLOUR

When joining in a new colour at the beginning of a round or middle of a row, work the last step of the stitch in the new colour. Catch the yarn in the new colour and draw through the loops on the hook to complete the stitch.

JOINING A NEW COLOUR
AT THE BEGINNING OF A ROUND

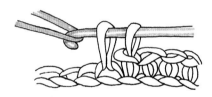

JOINING A NEW COLOUR
IN THE MIDDLE OF A ROW

CARRYING UNUSED YARN ACROSS THE WORK

When the colour that is not in use is to be carried across the wrong side of the work, it can be hidden along the line of stitches being made by working over the unused strand every few stitches with the new colour. This method is used for the Bengal cat (page 30). Lay the strand not being used on top of the previous row of stitches and crochet over it in the new colour, covering the unused colour.

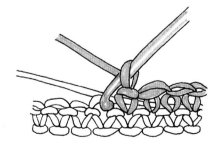

CARRYING UNUSED YARN
ACROSS THE WORK

Finishing Touches

HERE IS A GUIDE TO FINISHING YOUR PROJECT, FROM STUFFING AND SEWING THE CROCHETED PIECES TOGETHER TO EMBROIDERING THE DETAILS AND ADDING WHISKERS.

Stuffing

Polyester stuffing is a synthetic fibre that is lightweight and washable. It can also be found in black, which won't be so visible through the crocheted fabric in darker shades of yarn. Pure wool stuffing is a lovely, natural fibre. Durable and soft, it can be washed by hand but cannot be machine-washed as it will shrink and felt. Kapok is a natural fibre with a soft, silky texture. It comes from a seedpod that is harvested from the Ceiba tree.

Before stuffing your cat, tease the fibres by pulling them apart with your fingers to make them light and fluffy. Use small amounts at a time and line the inside of the crocheted fabric with a layer of stuffing before building up the filling in the centre. This will prevent the crocheted piece from looking lumpy.

Sewing the pieces together

When stitching up your work, use glass-headed dressmaker's pins to hold the pieces together. To join the legs to the body, flatten the tops and pin in position. Insert the needle through one stitch of the body, then through a stitch of the leg. Insert the needle into the body, a little further along, then into the leg again and draw up the yarn tightly. Work around the top of the thigh and under the body to attach the leg securely.

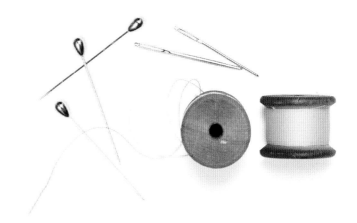

BACKSTITCH

This is a good method for sewing the cat's head to the body and attaching the ears and tail. Work close to the edges of the pieces for a neat finish.

Begin by working a couple of stitches over each other to secure the seam. Bring the needle through to the front of the work one stitch ahead of the last stitch made. Then insert the needle back through the work at the end of the last stitch. Repeat to complete the seam, making sure your stitches are neat.

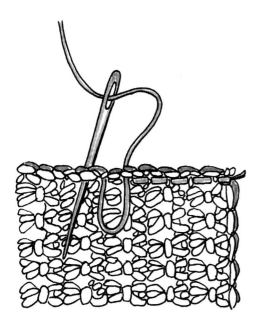

WHIP STITCH

Whip stitch is used to sew together the edges of most of the cats' tails. Thread the tail of yarn left after fastening off onto a blunt-ended yarn needle. With wrong sides of the tail together, insert the needle, from back to front, through a stitch on both sides at the same time and draw the yarn through the stitch. Insert the needle through the next stitch on both sides, from back to front, as before, and continue to the end. The yarn will be wrapped around the edges, joining the two sides.

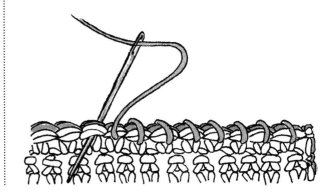

Embroidery stitches

Embroidered stitches are used to add the features and markings. The cats' eyes and noses are embroidered in satin stitch and short straight stitches. An embroidered fly stitch outlines the Maine Coon's nose (see page 65).

STRAIGHT STITCH

This is a single stitch that can be worked in varying lengths, which is useful for embroidering lines.

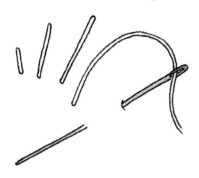

SATIN STITCH

Work straight stitches side by side and close together across a shape. Take care to keep the stitches even and the edge neat. The finished result will look like satin.

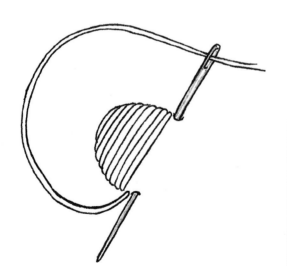

FLY STITCH

1 Bring the yarn through to the front of the work on the left side of the centre of the stitch and hold it down with your thumb. Insert the needle to the right, in line with the point where it first emerged. Bring the needle back through to the front of the work and a little way down, in line with the centre of the stitch, keeping the yarn under the needle.

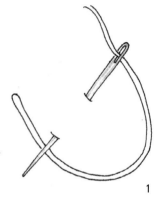

2 Pull the yarn through to form a V shape with the stitch. Insert the needle lower down, forming a straight line below the V-shaped stitch.

FASTENING OFF

To fasten off embroidery on the head or body, make a small knot in an area of the same colour where it won't show, or hide it where two pieces are joined, such as under the seam of the ear or behind the top of a leg. Weave in the ends.

Tassels

Tassels are used to create extra fur around the ruff of the Ragdoll cat, page 131, and the ear furnishings on the inner ears of the Ragdoll and also the American Bobtail, page 159. The strands of yarn or thread used can be trimmed to style.

To attach the tassel, fold the length of yarn in half to form a loop.

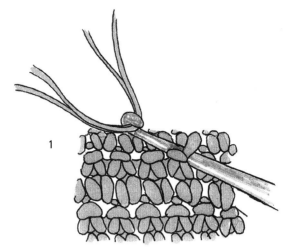

1 Insert crochet hook behind the post of the stitch and back out through to the front. Catch the looped yarn and pull a little way through.

2 Remove hook and thread ends of yarn back through the loop, pulling them tight. This completes one tassel.

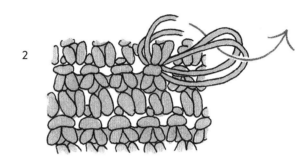

Whiskers

Clear nylon thread is used for the optional whiskers of each cat. This thread tends to work loose, so is not suitable for young children.
To give your cat whiskers, follow the instructions for attaching tassels.

171

Abbreviations

ch chain

cm centimetre(s)

dc double crochet

dc2inc work 2 double crochet stitches into the next stitch to increase

dc2tog work 2 double crochet stitches together to decrease

dc6tog work 6 double crochet stitches together to decrease

dc3inc work 3 double crochet stitches into the next stitch to increase

dec decrease

htr half treble

htr2tog work 2 half treble stitches together to decrease

in inches

inc increase

lp st loop stitch

m metre(s)

mb make bobble

mlb make large bobble

mm millimetre(s)

rep repeat

RS right side

sl st slip stitch

sp space

st(s) stitch(es)

tog together

tr treble

WS wrong side

yd yard(s)

yrh yarn round hook

* work instructions following the asterisks, repeating them as many times as directed

() repeat instructions inside brackets as many times as directed

Conversions

STEEL CROCHET HOOKS

UK	Metric	US
6	0.60mm	14
5½	–	13
5	0.75mm	12
4½	–	11
4	1.00mm	10
3½	–	9
3	1.25mm	8
2½	1.50mm	7
2	1.75mm	6
1½	–	5

STANDARD CROCHET HOOKS

UK	Metric	US
14	2mm	–
13	2.25mm	B/1
12	2.5mm	–
–	2.75mm	C/2
11	3mm	–
10	3.25mm	D/3
9	3.5mm	E/4
–	3.75mm	F/5
8	4mm	G/6
7	4.5mm	7
6	5mm	H/8
5	5.5mm	I/9
4	6mm	J/10
3	6.5mm	K/10.5
2	7mm	–
0	8mm	L/11
00	9mm	M–N/13
000	10mm	N–P/15

UK/US CROCHET TERMS

UK	US
Double crochet	Single crochet
Half treble	Half double crochet
Treble	Double crochet

Note: This book uses UK crochet terms

Suppliers

YARN

Drops Design
www.garnstudio.com

King Cole Ltd
www.kingcole.co.uk

LoveCrafts Group Ltd
www.lovecrafts.com

Purl Soho
www.purlsoho.com

Rowan
www.knitrowan.com

Scheepjes
www. scheepjes.com

Sirdar Spinning Ltd
www.sirdar.com

The Stitchery
www.the-stitchery.co.uk

Stylecraft
www.stylecraft-yarns.co.uk

Wool Warehouse
www.woolwarehouse.co.uk

CROCHET HOOKS

LoveCrafts Group Ltd
(see under Yarn)

Purl Soho
(see under Yarn)

The Stitchery
(see under Yarn)

Wool Warehouse
(see under Yarn)

TOY STUFFING

LoveCrafts Group Ltd
(see under Yarn)

Purl Soho
(see under Yarn)

Wool Warehouse
(see under Yarn)

World of Wool
www.worldofwool.co.uk

EMBROIDERY THREAD

Hobbycraft
www.hobbycraft.co.uk

Wool Warehouse
(see under Yarn)

Index

Acknowledgements

After writing *Crocheted Dogs*, it seemed only right to follow on with a book of crocheted cat patterns. Thank you Jonathan Bailey, Sara Harper, and all at GMC. Thank you to Jude Roust for checking the patterns, Anna Stevens and Andrew Perris for the lovely styling and photography, and to my wonderful, supportive family. Our present cat, Mavis, gave birth to her kittens at the bottom of a chest of drawers that my youngest had left open. Mavis' daughter, Birdie, lives with us, and her son, Brian, lives down the road with my eldest daughter, her family and their tabby, Babs. Brian is like a teddy bear and often comes up to visit, flopping down in front of our feet for a tummy rub. He's our favourite (don't tell the others).

I dedicate this book to my children, who persuaded us to welcome cats into our household over the years, and without whom we wouldn't have had Brian (or Mavis, Birdie and Babs) to inspire these projects.

First published 2023 by Guild of Master Craftsman Publications Ltd, Castle Place, 166 High Street, Lewes, East Sussex, BN7 1XU, UK.

Text and designs © Vanessa Mooncie, 2023
Copyright in the Work © GMC Publications Ltd, 2023

ISBN 978-1-78494-651-7

Reprinted 2024

PUBLISHER: Jonathan Bailey
PRODUCTION: Jim Bulley
SENIOR PROJECT EDITOR: Sara Harper
DESIGN MANAGER: Robin Shields
EDITOR: Nicola Hodgson
DESIGN: Rhiann Bull
PHOTOGRAPHER: Andrew Perris
STYLING: Anna Stevens
PATTERN CHECKING: Jude Roust
ILLUSTRATIONS & CHARTS: Vanessa Mooncie

Colour origination by GMC Reprographics
Printed and bound in China

To order a book,
contact:

GMC Publications Ltd
Castle Place, 166 High Street,
Lewes, East Sussex,
BN7 1XU
United Kingdom
Tel: +44 (0)1273 488005
www.gmcbooks.com